ENOUGH

as you are

ENOUGH
as you are

Overcoming Self-Doubt and
Appreciating the Gift of **YOU**

PEGGY WEBER

LOYOLA PRESS.
A JESUIT MINISTRY
Chicago

LOYOLA PRESS.
A JESUIT MINISTRY

3441 N. Ashland Avenue
Chicago, Illinois 60657
(800) 621-1008
www.loyolapress.com

Cover art credit: Irina Shisterova/iStock/Getty Images Plus/Getty Images

ISBN: 978-0-8294-4709-5
Library of Congress Control Number: 2019948170

Printed in the United States of America.
19 20 21 22 23 25 25 26 27 28 Versa 10 9 8 7 6 5 4 3 2 1

To my husband and best friend, John;
my children: Kerry, Matthew, and Elizabeth; and their
spouses: Colm, Nell, and Jeremiah;
and my AMAZING grandchildren: Marian, Cordelia,
Cillian, Jerome, Rose, Dominic, Brigid, and James Henry.

They fill my life with love, laughter, and inspiration.

Contents

Introduction

Sitting in church on Good Friday, my mind wandered, as it often does when I am in a quiet and reflective space. I began thinking of the prayer said at Mass before Communion—"Lord, I am not worthy that you should enter under my roof, but only say the word and my soul shall be healed." I say it so often, and my focus usually is on wanting to be healed from my sins, from my failings, and sometimes even from illness. But on this sacred day, I was dwelling on the words "I am not worthy." I suppose none of us feels worthy enough to have had Christ die for us, but that humbling thought can slide all too easily into self-doubt. On that afternoon, I realized that I have often felt that I truly was not worthy of this sort of love. I had always been taught that Jesus died for all of us, but did I really think that meant me, too? Part of me wondered whether God really knew what kind of person I was. Could he really love me that much to die for me? Did he truly understand all my flaws? If I believe that God knows everything—and I do—then he must see how I hold grudges. He must know that I worry too much and that I listen to gossip. And dear Lord, he must know that I am one of the most impatient people on the planet. Sitting in that pew, I was banking on being able to squeeze into the train car going to heaven and pray that no one asked for my ticket. I will try to be really quiet—that in itself will be a challenge—and I will pray, "Thank you, God, for dying on the cross for everyone here and maybe even me."

That experience in prayer made me consider how many times I have felt unworthy in my life, not just of God's love but of love from others, too, and how many times I have failed to love myself. So often, I have wondered whether I was smart enough, attractive enough, or cool enough. Daily, I would ask myself if I was a good enough writer, mom, wife, sister, or Catholic. I have worried about whether our family would have enough money and security, not trusting that we would somehow make it through, not trusting that God would care for us as a shepherd cares for his flock. To this day, the questions and doubts continue. I wonder if I did enough in my younger days to live now with good health. Why did I eat so much chocolate? Should I have filled out more crossword puzzles to keep my brain going?

I have wondered about all these questions and so many more. I have spent a lot of time wondering if I am any-number-of-things enough.

But on that day in church, somehow, through the grace of God, I realized I had the answer to all my worries in the very words of the question I was asking. I was right to focus on being enough. I just should have realized that to be "enough" for God, I need to be nothing more than my truest self, flaws and all. I should have figured out a long time ago that God loves even me and that, all along, *I am enough.*

Now, I have not spent every waking moment of my life feeling inadequate. But I want to share my struggles because I hope that in my doing so, others can avoid bearing the weight of the "enough-o-meter" I've been lugging around. As I enter the fourth quarter of life, it would be easy to look around and wonder if I have done enough, traveled enough, and even loved enough. But I have actually come to feel satisfied. I spend time with my grandchildren. I qualify for senior discounts. I am finally figuring things out. It is a struggle at times, but mostly I am content. And as I look back, I just want to wrap my arms around my younger self and say, "Fret not. You are fine. Don't waste your time worrying about whether you're worthy. You're already enough, as you are. You really are good enough—flaws and all. All of us are flawed. All of us are wonderful."

This lesson of contentment doesn't mean I plan to turn into a slug of self-satisfaction. We all can improve, learn, eat better, exercise more, pray more. But within the core of our being, we are enough today, this moment—not when you get a better job, not when you lose ten pounds—*right now*.

I hope this book can help you reflect on your own needs and insecurities and on what adopting a philosophy of *enough* can mean. I hope this book will help you explore why you might also be comparing yourself to others, feeling inadequate, or wondering if you are enough. I hope the book encourages you to embrace who you are, where you are, in an increasingly competitive, comparative, social media–centered world of FOMO (fear of missing out) and YOLO (you only live once). Along the way it is good to remember that we have help. In this book, as I have done in my life, I enlist the insights of some holy people—our saints. I am particularly struck by the forthright, simple wisdom of St. Francis de Sales, who stresses accepting yourself and choosing your own path to holiness. And at the end of each chapter I invite you to use the Examen questions. The Examen is a prayer technique created by St. Ignatius Loyola that offers daily reflection on God's presence in your life. I hope it helps guide you as you pray about being enough as you are.

The best part about knowing that we are enough is that we do not have to measure ourselves against the world and feel wanting. We can know that we are flawed people in need of love and assurance and also know that God already has given this to us in full measure.

1

Feeling Enough

Be who you are and be that perfectly well.
—St. Francis de Sales

For whatever reason you decided to read this book, thank you. We are beginning together to change the channel, so to speak, and listen to a voice with an affirming message about who we are. Are you ready? Are you hopeful? Are you willing to believe you are enough?

As you begin this book, you might want to grab a pad of paper and a pen. I like using a yellow legal pad and a fine-point, roller-ball pen. Perhaps you are high-tech and want to use your phone or tablet. Pick up whatever is useful to you. Now, make a list of five things you would like to do on a day off. This is not a bucket list. It's just a list of possibilities. Perhaps you want to take a hike or go to a movie or have lunch with a friend. You might even be practical and list catching up with laundry or grocery shopping.

How about buying a bathing suit? Did that make the list? Probably not. Most people do not feel excited about the chance to slip into polyester and spandex and stare at a full-length mirror that shows the body at every possible angle. When I have embarked on this task, I have rarely found myself twirling around, examining every inch in the three-way mirror and saying, "I love the way I look!" Bathing-suit shopping is just not a task that most people relish. A study at Flinders University in Australia found that even just imagining trying on a swimsuit can worsen a person's mood. It makes sense. I have heard the fittest people I know say something like, "I don't like my thighs." We always wish we had more muscles or more curves or a flatter stomach or a big T-shirt to cover everything up. Something always seems to be lacking.

When trying on a bathing suit, we're forced to scrutinize and to stare and to analyze ourselves, looking for potential flaws. And too often this is the sort of attitude we allow ourselves to adopt in other parts of our lives. Despite compliments, kind words, and maybe a lot of love from family and loved ones, we often are deeply critical of ourselves. And when we do receive praise, so often our inclination is to deflect it. How many times has a friend said to you, "Wow! I like your outfit. You look great!" and you replied: "Oh, I got this on sale. It was so cheap." Why can't we just say, "Thank you"? More importantly, it can be so hard to truly mean "thank you" and accept kind words.

Dancing in a Bathing Suit

While we adults can be weighed down by our insecurities, we also know that it was not always that way. Just spend some time with toddlers. They do not fret about a lot of the nonsense that takes up our time and causes us concern as adults. And when we witness this sort of self-confidence and lack of self-consciousness in toddlers, it can stick with us. One such memory of my youngest child still makes me feel as warm as the August afternoon when it occurred.

Our family was at my husband's company picnic at a local resort. Our three children had gone swimming, played shuffleboard, and gotten more than their fill at the ice-cream truck handing out free treats. There had been nonstop food and fun. Everyone was tired, and it was almost time to go home, but we stopped to listen to a DJ who was playing music at a pavilion. Our youngest, Elizabeth, who was two at the time, jumped right in and began dancing joyfully on the wooden floor. She was swirling and moving to the music and feeling the rhythm with her whole soul. I cannot recall what song was playing, but Elizabeth felt it. Swaying side to side and spinning about, our toddler was a lovely sight in her little pink bathing suit with ruffles. A professional photographer was snapping pictures of those attending the annual event. He took several photos of Elizabeth, who was having the time of her life as she pranced and jumped and smiled. There was no digital photography back then. These pictures were not instantly posted on Facebook or Instagram. Rather, we saw the photos about a month later when the company displayed some poster-sized pictures from the happy corporate event. And when the display was taken down, we were given the giant photo. We cherish it to this day.

In looking at the photo, you can see how Elizabeth radiates so much joy as she stands with her arms outstretched, making up her own dance. Her little belly sticks out. Her thighs are chubby. Her hair is askew from a day of swimming, playing, and now dancing. There are smears of ice cream and a bit of cotton candy on her face. She is so happy. And she is so beautiful. I remember how others on the dance floor commented on her lovely blue eyes and the sheer glee she showed as she moved around the floor. No one looked at this blue-eyed darling and said, "Oh, she is so cute, but her hair is a little messy." Nor did anyone say, "She would be even cuter if she were thinner." No one criticized her dance moves. The faces around her were smiling. People appreciated her just the way she was. And probably many of them wished that they, too, could feel that kind of freedom. This photo of our daughter dancing in her bathing suit represents more than our family history. It is a reminder of the desire to get back to that feeling, to that time when we quite literally danced as if no one were watching.

When Did You Stop Dancing?

Reflecting on these photos makes me wonder when, exactly, we start to care what others think—and why. When do we start to judge others rather than appreciate them? Why are we so hard on ourselves and others? What are the voices or influences that come into our lives and prevent us from being content? The beginnings of these feelings come at an early age. One study, explained in *The Confidence Code for Girls*, found that girls' confidence drops as much as 30 percent between the ages of eight and fourteen. Perhaps worry about being enough begins when we pay attention to advertisements that focus on how everyone looks. Maybe it is peer pressure that plants the seed of self-doubt. The pressure to fit in and be accepted starts alarmingly early; there are articles that promote having "the coolest backpack in kindergarten." Imagine if you pick the wrong kind. You already are on the "wrong" path at age five. And when kids get older, they feel they must have the latest and coolest kind of phone to go in the cool backpack. It's hard to grow up and fit in and figure out what matters.

But what about when you are past adolescence and into adulthood? You get to know yourself, and ideally you develop the ability to be happy with yourself. People still carry around the notion that everyone in the whole world has done more than they have or is doing it all better. Social media certainly does not help. Ultimately, you have to ask yourself, "What made me stop dancing in my bathing suit?" Perhaps we stop dancing when we begin to take to heart the myriad voices that surround us. How much weight do we give the voices that may come from advertisements, strangers, television shows, or friends? They can even begin when my little dancing toddler comes home from first grade and rejects the Barney and Friends lunch box that she carried proudly all through kindergarten. She no longer wants to bring it to school because someone at the lunch table said to her, "You still like Barney?! He's for babies." So Elizabeth asks for a generic lunch box or maybe an even safer brown bag to carry her meal. No one will know she still likes the purple dinosaur Barney. And so it starts. At age seven, criticism of a lunch box can make you feel less than enough.

All of us try to shake off the negative sounds. We try to listen to other, calmer, kinder, and more reassuring voices. The *Catechism of the Catholic Church* (listed on the Vatican website) says:

> **355** "God created man in his own image, in the image of God he created him, male and female he created them." Man occupies a unique place in creation: (I) he is "in the image of God"; (II) in his own nature he unites the spiritual and material worlds; (III) he is created "male and female"; (IV) God established him in his friendship.
>
> **357** Being in the image of God the human individual possesses the dignity of a person, who is not just something, but someone. He is capable of self-knowledge, of self-possession and of freely giving himself and entering into communion with other persons. And he is called by grace to a covenant with his Creator, to offer him a response of faith and love that no other creature can give in his stead.

Those are powerful words. We are made in God's image. We are not something but someone. Think about that. When your pants are too tight or you find a gray hair, remember that you are someone made in the image of God. Remember that when you feel that everyone else is at a party and you are not invited and sitting at home alone. And recall your dignity when voices hurt and say you are not good enough or do not look good enough. That message is clear when you realize people in the United States spend more than $60 billion each year trying to lose weight. This money goes to gym memberships, weight-loss programs, and diet foods and drinks. There's nothing wrong with striving to be healthy and to eat right, but most voices about weight loss go far beyond that. In fact, research shows that more than 65,000 national TV ads are aired each January and February by the weight-loss industry. That is a strong, loud, and persistent voice telling people to be thin! The message is clear: if you are thin, you will be happy. If you look good, you just might be enough. Is it any wonder so many young people develop eating disorders?

The voice that tells us to focus on how we look is not the same voice that reminds us we are made in the image of God. It is the collective voice of our culture that too often stresses appearance, from the men and women walking a red carpet to the selfies on someone's social media page. There are other voices in that chorus too. There are the voices that tell you that you need a nicer, faster, sleeker car. Still others promise you more fun and friends if you drink a particular beverage. It is hard not to come away with a list of the things that you supposedly need if you are going to *matter*.

For many years, the poster-sized photo of my daughter in her bathing suit sat in a closet. As adorable as it was, there did not seem to be a good place to hang it. But recently I pulled it out and framed it. We even used it as part of the decor for Elizabeth's thirtieth birthday party. That picture is the perfect reminder to me of a beautiful child who, then and now, is made in God's image and is full of love.

Do You Know That You Are Loved?

Happily, I continue to be inspired by the presence and personalities of my seven grandchildren, all age four and under. So often I look to these children to lead me. My oldest grandchild, four-year-old Cordelia, is the "dean of the cousins." She shows that same *joie de vivre* that her mother showed when she was twirling in her bathing suit. Cordelia, too, is happy to dance anywhere, anytime. She sings aloud for no reason. She says hello to everyone. And on a crisp fall day, she grabs my hand and points to the sky as a flock of geese passes overhead. We stop and stare and say, "Honk, honk, honk" and laugh as they fly by in a beautiful "V" formation. We are content and totally in that moment of awe. We are not thinking about what is to come or what mistakes we have made. We are not worried about someone hearing us honk. We are having fun. We are plain-old happy. It is a good feeling—one that all of us need to feel more often.

And at that moment, as I often do, I look at my granddaughter and say, "Who loves you, Cordelia?" She looks at me out of the corner of her eye and says, "Grandma." She knows it is the answer I expect. But she also knows that I will run by her side to swish through leaves and look at geese. And she knows that I will continue to run with her, come what may. There are no conditions. I just offer my love over and over again. And over and over again, she accepts it. She knows she is loved and lovable, and she offers the same love in return.

It should not be hard to love, but often it is. There is a vulnerability involved in loving that can keep us from being truly open and caring to others. And quite often it is hard to love one's own self. We are afraid that someone will find out who we really are, way down deep. Or we are afraid that we will be seen in an unfavorable light. How do we learn to love and achieve satisfaction when we are worn down or sad or lonely or just not feeling it? If you do not feel you are enough, then it is much harder to fully love and be loved.

Again, we can take a lesson from children. This time, think about how we allow ourselves to behave around them: We let down our defenses and make funny faces with kids. We look at a newborn with a sense of openness and wonder and awe. We stop and look up at the sky with a child and hope for geese. And of course, we then have to honk. We show appreciation when we are handed a dandelion bouquet. The joy children show around simple moments allows us to do the same. My grandson Jerome, when he was a baby, would sit in his highchair and eat his toast with gusto. He was so thrilled to have this warm, tasty food to gnaw. His smile and the way he savored his food made everyone smile and appreciate toast in all its glorious simplicity and plainness. We did not long for gourmet foods when looking at him. Rather, we just loved how much Jerome loved his toast.

Children also show us how to be open, especially with one another. My grandson Cillian loves machinery and trucks and anything with wheels. A highlight of his Wednesdays is watching the recycling truck come down the street. The workers wave to him and beep the horn on the truck. They, who have a very difficult job, smile and appreciate how much excitement they bring to a little boy's day. It is a happy time. They know that they have brought joy to a child.

We must make room for these still, small voices, these voices for good, that make their way into our days—the giggle of a child, the smile of a stranger, a nod in church, a pat on the back from a friend, a coworker's kindness, a hug from a loved one. And the more we listen to these, the more easily we can tune out those others that warn us about frizzy hair or advancing wrinkles that need a facial cream. We can stop hearing those voices that say we need to be married or single or working harder or earning more and trying to have it all—whatever "all" is! We must filter out those voices that tell us not to dance with joy in a pink ruffled bathing suit. When we filter out these voices, the only thing left is the voice of God, a God who wants us to recapture that childlike feeling of contentment, who tells us over and over again: "I love you. Do not measure yourself by your bank account or your car or your waist size." Let us listen to him. Let us focus on our breath, our being. Let us understand our dignity, our worth, and the ways we are made in the image of God. Understand that you are loved—just as you are.

Saintly Inspiration

St. Teresa of Ávila was a Carmelite nun in the sixteenth century. She learned to hear the voice of God through years of struggle as she became both a mystic and a reformer. Ultimately, she trusted God, and the prayer she wrote hundreds of years ago can still be seen in her own handwriting. The message resonates still today. She said, "Let nothing disturb you. Let nothing make you afraid. All things are passing. God alone never changes. Patience gains all things. If you have God, you will want for nothing. God alone suffices."

God and you are enough.

Putting Faith into Practice

- Make a list of five things you like about yourself.

- Accept a compliment—do not qualify it. Simply say thank you.

- Listen to the voices around you, including your own. Are they positive? Are they realistic? Are they honest?

- Look around and notice the people you admire. Why do you admire them? Identify a quality in these people that you can nurture in your daily life.

Ignatian Examen

Give thanks.

Thank you, Lord, for my life. It is not a perfect one, and I am not a perfect person, but I am grateful.

Ask for the Spirit.

Guide me, Lord, so that I can listen to the voices that matter. Help me tune out all the negative messages I receive about superficial things. I want to dance and sing as a child of God. Help me.

Review and recognize challenges and failures.

God, help me to not be too hard on myself. Help me see myself as a flawed but good person. Do I recognize that I will make mistakes? Do I accept that I may gain weight, say the wrong thing, or mess up, and even so, I am still worthy of love?

Ask for forgiveness and healing.

Lord, help me appreciate my gifts and talents and rejoice in how "fearfully and wonderfully" I have been made (Psalm 139). Forgive me for all the times I have been negative about myself. Help me listen to the "right" voices and discern what truly matters.

Pray about tomorrow.

Lord, help me focus on being enough because I am your child. Show me how to value myself.

2
Friends Enough

It is wonderful how attractive a gentle, pleasant manner is, and how much it wins hearts.

—St. Francis de Sales

Time to make another list. Write down the names of five good friends. You don't have to rank them or tell them they made the list. But think of these people when you read this chapter and ask yourself why they are your friends. Then think about letting them know how much you appreciate them. It feels good to belong. It feels good to have friends. It feels good to be a good friend.

Friends Matter

The word *friend* evokes a lot of feelings, images, and memories and holds many different meanings for people. You might use the term loosely and call lots of people friends; you may have thousands of Facebook friends, for example. Or perhaps you use the term *friend* for a few select people. However you define *friend*, you probably believe that friends are an important part of life, providing comfort, counsel, and companionship.

Scripture reinforces the idea that friends matter. The book of Sirach says: "Faithful friends are a sturdy shelter: whoever finds one has found a treasure. Faithful friends are beyond price; no amount can balance their worth. Faithful friends are life-saving medicine; and those who fear the Lord will find them" (Sirach 6:14–16).

When we are young, the act of making friends can seem so easy. My little granddaughter, Cordelia, uses the term *friend* generously. She sees everyone she meets as either her friend or a potential friend. And I do mean everyone. During the 2018 Winter Olympics in South Korea, Cordelia was very excited about the games. I mentioned to her that a friend of her mother's was living in South Korea. She liked that she knew someone who lived there. Then she asked, "And do we know anyone in North Korea?" I should have said no. But I replied with the only name I knew: "Just Kim Jong-un." I was being a bit sarcastic and silly as I said the name of the Supreme Leader of North Korea. Cordelia, in all her innocence and sweetness, did not understand. She just said, "Is he our friend?" When I said no, she looked concerned. "Why isn't he our friend?" In her world, if you know someone, that person is your friend. I should never have been so cavalier in my response. And her genuine openness to being friends with everyone around the globe, even dictators, reminded me that friendship is a deep and natural need, but one that it is all too easy to close ourselves off from. My conversation with Cordelia also reminded me how much more complicated the idea of friendship can become as we grow older.

Friendship, in theory, is simple. When my children were in kindergarten, their teacher told their class, "You can't say 'You can't play.'" She stressed inclusiveness and worked hard to create a class in which all were welcome. It worked, most of the time. Early childhood can be a safe and happy time for friendship. Looking back, I realize that I had a snug and good life at home. I had friends, and I liked school. I took Irish step-dancing lessons with my cousin. My brother and I delivered more than a hundred newspapers each night to neighborhood homes. I read—a lot. And I spent just about as much time in church as I did with my beloved books. Everyone on our street played together. There were nightly games of kick the can or some other sport or game. Being one of the younger kids in our neighborhood, I was happy just to be a part of it all. And the big kids were kind enough to include us. I belonged. I had community.

But in seventh grade, life changed quite a bit, especially when it came to my understanding of friendship. My best friend since the second grade stopped hanging out with me. There was no conversation or explanation. It just happened. The cool girls invited her into their circle, and that meant I was no longer invited to her house or included in her conversations at recess. My books, my homelife, and the kids on the street were still there for me, but in terms of this friendship I was at a loss. I tried to find new friends. I tried to fit in. Yet, I faltered. Nothing clicked.

The culmination of my junior high years came on the day of the eighth-grade field trip. Our class was heading to a local amusement park. We climbed on the bus and everyone found a seat with someone. Well, everyone but one. I looked around and saw that the numbers were not even, which meant that I had to sit alone. In fairness, I am sure many of my classmates might not have even noticed me that day. They were content with their seatmates, happy to have a partner, and excited about our day out of school. Most were probably thinking about snacking on treats or riding the roller coaster. But it was in that moment, standing alone in the aisle of the bus, when I, for the first time, began to feel that maybe I was not enough.

I found a seat and bounced along on the yellow school bus and stared out the window. I felt a bit like a leper. And I began to think that maybe my situation was not just a result of an odd number of girls. Perhaps I was an odd person. I knew that I was not one of the cool girls and had no aspirations to be part of the in-crowd. They did not share my interest in reading dozens of books about World

War II. And they probably owned more records than I did in my collection of one: *Glen Miller's Greatest Hits*. I can see now that I was different, but on the bus that day I felt not just different but *insufficient*. Strangely enough, I do not remember too much about the rest of the day. I know that some kids let me tag along with them, and I made it through the amusement park even though I certainly did not feel amused. Though I can recall the experience of being left out, my personal resiliency kicked in, and I moved on to high school. I told myself that grammar school was done, and I was ready to move toward better times. And I did, thanks to making some good friends.

Feeling Accepted Enough

Friendship truly is a blessing. There may be people who have never felt bad about themselves or have never experienced rejection. However, I think most people have at least felt anxious about a new experience and wondered if they would fit in or be liked. Have you ever tried to make new friends? Maybe it was when starting at a new job or a new school. Do you remember what it felt like to join a new parish or move to a new place to live? This feeling of wanting to belong and hoping that you are enough is not just limited to eighth graders sitting on a bus.

We've all been there, even for a short time. Did you ever walk into a meeting or conference and feel as if everyone but you was doing great? Have you ever asked to sit at a table and been told the seats were saved—in situations far beyond high school? Have you ever looked around a room and wondered why you weren't enjoying yourself? And have you ever wanted to shout, "Hello! I am here! I'm nice too!"?

There's nearly always someone in the room who needs a helping hand, a smiling face, or a seat at the table. Most of us get into comfortable routines, with our group of friends, and we don't always notice the new person or the lonely person. I think the pain and sorrow I experienced in eighth grade after that experience on the bus helped me grow in compassion for others. It enabled me to recognize and reach out to others who may be feeling alone. If you have felt left out, you understand. That feeling of not fitting in also makes you treasure the feeling of finding and making a good friend, because friends are important. They matter.

Even science tells us that friends can make a world of difference. A recent study at the University of Virginia took a group of students to the bottom of a hill. They were given heavy backpacks and asked to guess how steep the hill was. Those who stood with friends thought the hill would be easier to climb. The closer the friendship, the easier the climb looked. Those who stood alone thought the hill would be much steeper and more challenging. The lesson: life is easier when you have someone by your side.

When you reach out or when someone reaches out to you, grace abounds. Good things often happen in those moments. A few months after that lonely ride on my class trip, I headed to high school. I began to encounter lots of great kids who liked me as I was. I fit in with a group of kids. It did not happen right away, but I remember the thrill of being handed an invitation to a party. My lab partner gave me a card after the end of class. She said she thought I was funny and wanted to include me on her guest list. I was thrilled to be invited to Nora's house. I remember going home and showing my mother the invitation and practically preening like a rooster as I walked around the kitchen and discussed the big event. My joy was obvious, and it brought me to a deeper understanding of how friendship can boost your spirit, your sense of self.

Through the years, I have also realized how important it is to be a good friend and share an invitation or a kindness. It is such a good feeling to be invited. Having a sense of being welcomed matters. A nice greeter at a parish can put a smile on your face as you enter church. Smiling and nodding at a person who is new to a meeting or an event or a parish function can change that person's whole experience. And a single act of kindness can make a big difference. In fact, a single kind decision by relative strangers changed my entire college experience.

God's grace intervenes—or one might call it divine providence.

I was a happy, excited but nervous college freshman. I hoped that the next four years would be as good as people said college could be. It represented a world of possibilities for my seventeen-year-old self. Some boys from my high school class had enrolled in my college, but I did not know a single female student on campus. I had high hopes, but I also felt totally on my own.

When the first Saturday night on campus arrived, I was grateful when my college roommate and some of her high school friends invited me to join them. Once again, I was happy just to be tagging along, to be included.

Back then, the drinking age was eighteen. With our newly minted college IDs, we went to the campus bar. None of us wanted to drink much; we hoped we might talk with some boys. A senior was at the door checking everyone's credentials. We were giddy with excitement and wondering what our first big social experience would be like. The young man at the door waved us through but added casually, "And you're all eighteen, right?" Everyone nodded but me. My October birthday was a month away. I could not lie. I told him that I was not quite eighteen but that I only wanted a soda. He shook his head and told me I had to leave. How foolish I felt! Who starts their college social life by getting kicked out of a bar at 8 p.m. for being too young and too honest? I expected that my new group of friends would wave goodbye to me and I would go back to my dorm to read and probably cry. I imagined myself doing homework while others partied. But the young women I was with didn't say goodbye. They left the bar with me. I was astonished. They barely knew me, but they did not ditch me. They did, justifiably, tease me about the experience. "I only want a Coke," they mimicked playfully. But they stuck by me. I cannot recall what we did the rest of the night. We wandered around the campus a bit and probably ended up back in a dorm room chatting. I got to know them and discovered they were funny and nice and loyal. One of those gracious, kind women, Beth, is still one of my dearest friends. Those young women did not have to be that nice. They did not have to be kind or inclusive, but they were. It was a great way to begin my college life, and it set the tone for the next four years. During those years at college, I felt that I was enough, in part because I made such good friends that night. And because of experiencing that kindness, I vowed to try to be a good enough friend to others.

Appreciating Friends

Perhaps you have felt the joy of a good friend, or maybe you have endured the pain of being left out. The experiences of being both included and excluded have stayed with me in significant ways. Knowing what it is like to sit alone makes me far more compassionate toward others. The sense of being alone and lonely makes me realize how important it is for people to feel that they belong in order to feel that they are enough. You cannot feel good if you feel left out. And I would think that you shouldn't feel good if you are leaving out others. It is not enough to know that you have your circle of friends. Finding that group where you belong is great. But we should not simply attend a party or walk into a parish hall or sit on the sidelines of a child's soccer game without looking around and consciously inviting others in.

My family jokes that I will talk to anyone, and I suppose it's true. So I use my chatty nature to reach out. I believe that everyone should feel welcome, whether at church, out in the neighborhood, or in line at the grocery store. Kindness matters. In fact, my mother often said to me that "a kindness is always remembered." And it often is in the small gestures that kindness is felt and differences are made. My son and nephew were the altar servers at my father's funeral. The boys, ages ten and nine, were sad and also a bit scared about carrying out their duties. After the funeral Mass, they came out of the sacristy with grins. One of the nice celebrants had told them they had done a good job and offered them each a stick of gum. They lapped up the praise and the treat and felt much better while going through a difficult day. To this day, the boys remember the priest and appreciate his kind words and actions.

I haven't always been the perfect friend, but I try to stay connected and to sustain meaningful relationships. Sometimes it is just a matter of letting someone know I am thinking of him or her. I like to bake cookies or Irish bread or brownies for friends. And my husband, who can fix just about anything, shows support to his friends by helping them make repairs on their homes or cars. A dear friend of mine used to send cards to all three of my children for every major holiday (and several minor ones!). We joked that she kept card companies in business. They loved it, and I loved how kind she was to them. There is no perfect way to be a good friend, but we can practice what we know and also imitate what others have done in their friendship toward us.

I have come a long way from that lonely bus ride in eighth grade and from that scene at the campus bar. I look back now and see that the young girl, the young me, was definitely enough. She just didn't know it yet.

Saintly Inspiration

Acts of friendship span a wide spectrum. People help in small, daily ways. Or they help in big ways, like giving you a place to live or driving you hundreds of miles to see a sick parent. Then there are dramatic examples of friendship, such as donating a kidney. Or risking your life.

St. Maximilian Kolbe was the ultimate friend. In July 1941, he was a prisoner in the Auschwitz concentration camp. Ten prisoners escaped, so the commander of the camp picked ten men to starve to death. He wanted to punish the remaining prisoners and deter them from planning further escapes. It is reported that one of the ten selected cried, "My wife! My children!" Upon hearing this, Maximilian Kolbe volunteered to take his place. Eyewitnesses report that this saintly man, for two weeks, led his fellow prisoners in prayer as they awaited their death.

Kolbe knew what friendship meant when he wrote to Polish friars in 1940: "A single act of love makes the soul return to life. Let us often make use of this means."

Putting Faith into Practice

- Recall when a friend made a difference in your life.
- Send a note or pick up the phone to thank a friend for support and love.
- Take the time to look around your workplace, neighborhood, parish, or even your home and try to see who needs a little extra kindness or a smile. Then give it.

Ignatian Examen

Give thanks.

Thank you, Lord, for friends. Thanks for the kindred spirit who shares a cup of tea with me. Thanks for the friend who makes me laugh. Thank you for the cherished memories of fun times. Thank you for the friend who comforts me during sorrow.

Ask for the Spirit.

Ask the Holy Spirit to help you appreciate the incredible joy that comes from friendship. Pray for help in noticing friends and not taking them for granted. Appreciate your friends who love you, warts and all.

Review and recognize challenges and failures.

Consider how you can be a better friend. Reflect on how you can be a better listener. Ask yourself if you use the "I'm so busy" excuse too often. Think about what matters—friends and family—and then make time for them. Try to see the good in people and appreciate them as they are. And try to appreciate yourself and know that you are worthy of friends, just the way you are.

Ask for forgiveness and healing.

Think about what you could do to be more inclusive. Have you ignored others and been content with your own crowd, your group, your life? Try to see others around you as people who just want some encouragement.

Pray about tomorrow.

Lord, help me value the gift of friendship. Help me feel good enough about myself as a person and friend. Help me do a little something extra to be a truly good friend. Lord, let me never forget that you are my friend, who certainly has done unbelievable things for me.

3
Smart Enough

Don't get upset with your imperfections. It's a great mistake because it leads nowhere—to get angry because you are angry, upset at being upset, depressed at being depressed, disappointed because you are disappointed. So don't fool yourself. Simply surrender to the Power of God's Love, which is always greater than our weakness.
—St. Francis de Sales

Ready to use the pad and pencil again? Imagine you have a "smart-o-meter," and give yourself a grade from 1 to 10: How smart are you? Are you a 5? Does that mean you are average? Did you write a 10? Or a 1? And how do you measure being smart? If you can answer these questions with ease and a smile, you may be on your way to seeing that you are smart enough.

Who Likes the Renaissance?

On a hot September night, I sat in my first college class, looked around the room, and wondered if anyone was as anxious as I was. I felt warm in my new college clothes and a bit weird since I had worn uniforms for the first twelve years of my schooling. Twenty eager, earnest faces looked at one another, but no one spoke. We waited, a circle of both worry and hope, and listened as the professor began to speak. This was no ordinary class, where we could sit passively and take notes. This was a seminar in my college honors program, and I was pretty sure I would have to say something. Dear God, what could I say? I should have been excited. I should have felt happy to be part of a wonderful program. Instead, I wondered if everyone else in the room had pearls of wisdom waiting to come out of their mouths while I could think of nothing to contribute. Actually, saying nothing might not be too bad compared with saying something dumb. I wondered if they would look at me and determine that I was not smart enough.

Feeling so insecure should have seemed silly. After all, the college invited me to be part of its program. They must have figured that I could do the work. But those kids in that circle in that seminar looked really, really smart. One boy had a beard and gestured with his glasses. He must be intelligent, I thought. He talks already as if he's a professor. At that moment I did not thank God for my good eyesight; instead, I wanted glasses. I wanted to gesture with glasses in the hopes that it would make me look smarter. And although I did not wish for a beard, I really thought the whiskers on some of my male classmates made them look far more knowledgeable than I was. It was especially effective when they stroked their beards before speaking, as if they had just come up with another great idea.

Our professor was an enthusiastic Dominican priest who looked at all of us with both friendliness and amusement as he asked us to introduce ourselves and describe one of our interests. There was nothing unreasonable about such a request. In theory the question was simple, but I quickly began to wonder what my answer might imply. Should I say something that might impress my classmates or my professor? Or should I just tell the truth?

The circle of smart answers began. Some students mentioned that they were interested in music or languages or science. And then the girl next to me offered the smartest-sounding answer yet.

"I'm interested in the Renaissance," she said sincerely. Our professor seemed a bit surprised but smiled. "Really, what part of the

Renaissance?" he asked. She was quite confident as she replied, "Oh, the Italian Renaissance." She was not putting on airs. Her father was a professor. She spoke Italian. She had been to Italy. And she really liked the era's art, music, and architecture. Now I knew the word *renaissance*, but I was not sure I could spell it. And I had no idea what it meant or how any person my age could already be interested in it. Right then and there, I determined I was not up to snuff with this crowd. I had never met anyone in my whole life who was interested in the Italian Renaissance. I did, though, love spaghetti. Should I say that?

Finally, it was my turn. So I just looked at the nice priest and said, "I am interested in baseball, specifically the Boston Red Sox." He smiled, but I did not think he looked impressed. I was probably being a bit sarcastic because I was so intimidated. However true the answer was, I still felt it was insufficient. I wondered later what else I could have said. What response could I have given that would have made me look like I fit into this new and smart world?

I concluded that day that although I was a good student and happy to learn, I was not as smart as most of the people in that room. When they talked about opera, I figured it was not for me. When they mentioned going to a serious play, I preferred to see a musical. When they talked about going to museums and admiring art, well, I went to basketball games and watched my friends run cross-country races.

I had decided that smart people did certain things, and I did not do any of them. I made up my mind that I was not smart enough to be part of that group. Years later, I realize how foolish I was. I clumped certain subjects into a category and stayed away from them, assuming they weren't for me. I have now visited many museums and attended classical music events, and I appreciate their beauty. But there still is a little discomfort as I fear that someone will see I do not understand the meaning of a great painting or the history behind a concerto. I still feel that I do not belong in the deep end of the pool. There are days when I am not sure I should even be in the shallow end and think the kiddie pool is the best fit for me.

Tough on Yourself

Perhaps this has happened to you. Perhaps at one point you felt foolish or you failed at something and berated yourself for not being smart enough. Can you recall that feeling? It's not a good one. But honestly, it is an understandable one. We all feel wanting when we measure ourselves against the person who got a 100 when we got a 90—or perhaps we think we are the only person who ever failed an exam.

Perhaps you measure intelligence by a person's achievements in school. School does take up a large portion of life, including our most formative years. Yet our own experience teaches us that "school smarts" do not account for all of the intelligence we gain throughout a lifetime.

We know as we grow that every person is gifted in his or her own way. What are your own skills, abilities, and intelligence? How much do you value them? How much do you believe in yourself and your "smarts"?

There are various reasons we may not have confidence in our own intelligence. It might stem from our youth. My school had unique but sometimes difficult reminders that some kids were "brighter" than others. One teacher in my grammar school had the students sit according to their report-card average. I never had that teacher, but if I brought a note to her class, I knew right away how every kid was ranked. First seat, first row: those kids were the smart ones. That last row near the windows: well, we knew where they ranked. Imagine what that system did to a lot of children sitting in that formation for a year! And reading groups could be a revelation. You knew where you stood after the sorting was done. If you were in the Blessed Mother reading group, you had a good grasp of the subject. If you were in the St. Jude reading group, you had a ways to go.

When papers were handed back in school, I always looked for a sticker to see if I had done well. When I was little, the teachers put stickers on our uniforms or even our foreheads if we had made the grade in school. I wore those stickers with pride as I went home, but I know now that not everyone got a sticker, nor did everyone thrive in that mode of education. My stickers were awarded because I had memorized my catechism questions. However, I realize now that what I enjoyed must have been hard for others. I had been blessed with a good memory and could recite in front of the class. Other students might have known the answers but had trouble remembering immediately, and others probably froze when asked questions.

School suited me, but I can see where many would feel "less than" during some of the lessons. For me, spelling bees were fun. Shouting out the answers to multiplication problems was kind of fun. However, art class was never, ever fun. And to this day, I cannot read music, even though I enjoy singing. I would stare at the notes on the scale and know they went up and down but could never call out their names, never mind whether flat or sharp. I clearly was not sharp in that department, but fortunately that did not hold me back. But I imagine how I would have struggled if I could not read and how difficult school would have been for me if words were as jumbled as musical notes.

The classroom can be a difficult place for so many. Today, most educators practice a more enlightened approach to the way they teach and reward students. Educators understand that children have different learning styles and thrive best when teachers meet them where they are and as they are. It is good to recognize, even now, that all of us—whether we think we are smart or dumb or in-between—learn differently and have unique talents.

Recognize Your Gifts and Talents

My father couldn't read music either—not a note. However, it did not hold him back as a musician. He played in his college band and was a hit at most parties as he delighted the crowd with his piano playing. He played by ear and was very gifted. It was remarkable to watch him sit down and just play any song that was requested. He is the perfect example of someone who was smart in a unique way. I also have met people who can just paint or draw or speak foreign languages with ease. And there are those who handle math without difficulty. So many gifts and talents require a particular kind of intelligence. Some people have the capacity to say the right thing in a tough situation or to simply listen in a compassionate way. Others have a gift of style and know how to dress or design a room. People can be "smart" in so many different ways. However, many people do not get that message and just think that report cards or SAT scores have defined them.

Howard Gardner of the Harvard Graduate School of Education wrote a book in 1983 called *Frames of Mind: The Theory of Multiple Intelligences*. I do not presume to understand all of it, but he explained that a person should not see intelligence as dominated by a single general ability. In other words, there are lots of ways to be smart. Other studies have indicated that, if teachers have high expectations of their students, then the students will learn more and perform better. Attitude matters so much when it comes to the learners and how they perceive themselves and how they are perceived.

Of course, each of us does not necessarily have the ability to become a brain surgeon. But just think for a moment about how you feel about yourself when you reflect on the word *smart*. Does it make you feel good? Do you think you are intelligent and capable and able to take on the world? Some may offer a tentative yes, and a few may be very confident, but most of us have, at least to a degree, placed limits upon ourselves that are based on flawed perceptions and a feeling that we have never been smart enough.

This attitude can be especially harmful when it comes to learning about our faith. For example, it is easy to fall into the trap of thinking that learning about God is limited to those with degrees in theology or those who hold positions in the church. But family members are important too.

I know that my faith was nurtured by and passed down from my grandmother, who came to the United States from Ireland with a very limited education and a great love for God. She opened her heart and front door to all in need and raised her daughters, including my mother, to love others. My mother, whose education did not extend beyond high school, was one of the wisest and smartest people I ever met. One of her bits of advice has stayed with me for a long time: "I don't go to church for Father, I go for God." I had come home from school and told my mother that a parishioner was leaving our parish because she was mad at our pastor. Well, my mother set me straight, and her statement has often kept me focused on what really matters regarding my faith and my attitude toward the institutional church. She helped me see that although a good priest can certainly help a parish, the personality of the priest is not the main reason to go to church. My mother's theology and understanding of the importance of the Eucharist and her faith were impressive. She had no degree letters after her name, but she certainly taught, in words and actions, what it meant to be a committed Catholic.

None of this is meant to dismiss learning or continuing education. My mom participated in retreat programs, attended talks and missions, and read Catholic publications. She taught me that continuous learning was important. But she also showed me that learning is a gift and not something to be used to intimidate others. She and my dad also showed me that intelligence comes in many forms and that all gifts and talents—whether gardening or calculus or music or languages or art or community building—contribute to our world.

And yet so many of us continue to measure ourselves by our accomplishments in school or our lack of them. Many do not recognize that, no matter their test scores, they are, as the Scriptures say, "made in the image and likeness of God."

In a July 2013 speech by Pope Francis to Muslims throughout the world, the pontiff sent a message of good wishes upon the end of Ramadan. He wrote:

> What we are called to respect in each person is first of all his life, his physical integrity, his dignity and the rights deriving from that dignity, his reputation, his property, his ethnic and cultural identity, his ideas and his political choices. We are therefore called to think, speak and write respectfully of the other, not only in his presence, but always and everywhere, avoiding unfair criticism or defamation. Families, schools, religious teaching and all forms of media have a role to play in achieving this goal.

I love this statement because it emphasizes that everyone should be valued, and being valued extends far beyond the classroom. For example, an elderly person who has dementia has value. It is painful to watch someone you love lose cognitive abilities; still, that person has value. Again, I go back to my beloved mother. She had a serious stroke and struggled greatly to speak. It was painful to watch her try to form words. Yet, even if she never spoke another word, she mattered to me. I sat with her every day, and as she caressed my cheek, I knew what she was trying to communicate. She wanted me to know I was loved, even if she could not say the words.

Any child with disabilities should be treasured. It was frightening to read the many news stories reporting that Iceland has practically "eliminated" Down syndrome from its society through abortion. It seemed to celebrate that this genetic abnormality would no longer exist. There was an outcry from families who had members with Down syndrome; they stressed the value that their family members bring to the world. And people with Down syndrome wrote to newspapers and expressed their own outrage. What measuring stick do we use to value people?

Saintly Inspiration

Imagine living in a world that tells you that you do not matter because you cannot do something well. You are told you are not smart enough and made to feel you are not good enough. St. André Bessette, canonized in 2010, probably heard those words a few times in his life. He entered the Holy Cross Brothers in Montreal, Canada, in 1870. He was twenty-five, had no formal education, and had a history of poor health. He did laundry, was a messenger, and became a porter who answered the door and took care of the mail. He did those tasks for forty years. Most would not see this as a path to greatness—never mind sainthood. But he also prayed with many people who came to the door. His prayers and counsel were associated with many healings. He also helped build an oratory to St. Joseph. When he died in 1937 at age ninety-one, it was estimated that one million people went to the chapel to pay their respects to this holy man.

St. André Bessette's words remind us not to worry but to concentrate on this: "Put yourself in God's hands; He abandons no one."

Putting Faith into Practice

- Make a list of at least three gifts or talents you have. Thank God for them and take a moment to appreciate them.

- Add to your list. Name three ways you would like to expand your skills or knowledge. Then plan how to begin. Maybe you want to learn to knit or take photos or speak in public. Do it. You do not have to be perfect.

- Then, tell three people what gifts or abilities you appreciate in them. Praise matters. And if you want, give your friends a sticker!

Ignatian Examen

Give thanks.

Thank the Lord for your intelligence—your ability with words, numbers, art, music, farming, building, cooking, encouraging, and so on. Do not dwell on what you cannot do but express your gratitude for what you can do.

Ask for the Spirit.

Ask the Lord for the resolve to keep on learning and to appreciate educational opportunities that can benefit you. Ask for the wisdom to see that everyone learns at his or her own pace and in his or her own way.

Review and recognize challenges and failures.

Have you criticized your own intelligence recently? If so, why? Are you being too hard on yourself or looking at yourself with an unrealistic perspective? How can you train yourself to better recognize your gifts and the gifts of others?

Ask for forgiveness and healing.

Ask God to help you understand and appreciate the brilliance of others and be glad for who you are and the gifts you have. If you want to learn more and improve, do so. But look at learning as a joy, not a measuring stick. Appreciate all people, of all ages and abilities. Forgive yourself and forgive those who have made you feel less than you are.

Pray about tomorrow.

Try this prayer: Dear Lord, I may not be able to understand everything. But I am yours, a child of God, and made in your image. I thank you for my abilities and ask to be able to use them well for the good of myself and others.

4
Loved Enough

You learn to speak by speaking, to study by studying, to run by running, to work by working, and just so, you learn to love by loving. All those who think to learn in any other way deceive themselves.

—St. Francis de Sales

Prepare to write or type; we are ready to think about *love*. That word can mean so much. To help sort things out a bit, write "Love is . . ." and offer a few answers. Perhaps love is eating a warm chocolate-chip cookie with your child. Or maybe love is donating your coat to a clothing drive. Or love might be your husband or wife or parent or some other family member. Whatever it is, love is something we all need.

Hold My Hand

"Hand, hand, hand!" I heard this often when my grandson Cillian was beginning to talk. He would reach out with his sweet, sometimes sticky little fingers and then lead me toward something. Usually he directed me to a toy, a book, or some food. And then I would look at the train or Play-Doh or Cheerios or truck book and see what he wanted. Then he would say, "Sit, sit, sit." He did not just want me to see the object of his great interest from afar. He wanted me at his level, right next to him, so that he could show me more closely what it was that had captured his interest. He wanted me to look at his amazing cement mixer or to squish clay with my fingers or to admire his picture—all from his viewpoint. He wanted me to be present to him. He wanted me right there and involved. He did not want to have me looking down at his item of interest and not really paying attention. He did not want just a nod or a pat on the head from me. He did not want a small gesture from the sofa that required no effort. No, he wanted it all. He wanted me on the rug and shoulder to shoulder. He wanted me to be able to look him in the eye and understand. He wanted to get me to really see the truck or the ball or the story of an owl or the yummy snack. He wanted my time and focus. He wanted commitment. He wanted me. He wanted my love.

Of course I gave it to him. And as I have watched him grow up, I have seen that he is just a big sponge who wants to absorb love and learning. He communicates much more easily now, but his message is the same. He wants me to pay attention and be with him. With his sweet blue eyes and adorable smile, he asks me, "Grandma, read book? Grandma come upstairs and play trucks?" He is open and honest about his need for love. And instinctively he knows that he will get it from me, the grandparent who thinks he is absolutely amazing. Although he is just a little boy, he is like all of us who just want to be loved enough by someone special. He is clear and forthright. "I need you. I want you. I love being loved," he says in so many ways. He is a great teacher to me about what it means to give of oneself.

Love can be complicated and risky when you are older. You wonder if you should let another person know that you care. You wonder if it is worth making the extra effort for another. You might get hurt. You probably will get hurt somewhere along the line. *Is it really better to have loved and lost?* you wonder. But, again, Cillian is a teacher.

One evening I was putting him to bed, and he was quite restless. It was a rare occasion for me to do this, and he wanted the routine and comfort of his folks. His devoted parents are almost always home, but on this night I was in charge of bath, bedtime story, and sleep. He had already told me with a sigh, "I miss Mommy! I miss Daddy!" I told him that I understood that he missed them but they would be home soon. He nodded and seemed to realize that I was all he had at that moment. He sighed again. But then he looked at me and said, "Big hug!" I complied happily and told him I loved him. This helped, evidently; he fell asleep. I guess I would do for the time being, and I was glad that he settled down and settled for me as a substitute. This experience is a tender memory for me. But it is more than that. It showed me how, from young age to old age, the need for a hug, for reassurance, for love, is very real. It is a powerful need that never ends.

All of us need to be loved. Sometimes we dismiss that need, but it remains. Whether through friendship, marriage, a religious vocation, or devotion to family, we desire to love and be loved. We try to fill this need in many ways, try to figure out what is good, what is enough. Some of us seek love through websites, noisy bars, volunteer work, or hobbies. The search can be tricky. Sometimes it seems that if we go looking for love or try too hard to find a special relationship, it won't happen. At other times, when we least expect it, love might just drop in. But most of the time, it requires being vulnerable. It means asking someone to take your hand and sit. It can be amazing, but it can hurt. It truly is a mystery. And it can be hard.

Love Is a Challenge

Love requires commitment, something that isn't always easy or always present in a relationship. The divorce rate hovers around 50 percent, indicating that marital love obviously has challenges. The numbers of those committing to religious life and the priesthood are down. Committing to love can be scary, and fewer people seem willing to take that plunge. And in a world that seems busier and more hectic each day, we discover that we have less time for friends and family. It can make you wonder if real love is possible anymore. It can make you wonder how you know when love is real. How do you know when it is worth putting out your hand? I do not have a perfect answer. However, the advice I was given by a good Dominican priest in college has stayed with me and helped me sort out what it means to be loved enough.

The priest was teaching a seminar on T. S. Eliot, but often the class discussion went beyond poetry. He would talk about religious life, faith, and figuring out what we students were going to do with our lives. Naturally, the topic of marriage came up. He looked at us and asked, "Beyond the talk of love, what is an important question you should ask about your future spouse? Remember you are giving yourselves to each other." Many answers were offered, but several centered on the idea that you should ask if you were worthy of and committed enough toward your intended. The priest surprised us when he said adamantly, "No! What you should ask is if your intended is worthy of you. It is not arrogance. You are giving the most precious gift you can give: yourself. Do not squander it. Be sure that your future spouse is worthy of you."

Those words have stayed with me for decades. The priest's message was simple: Don't settle for just any life or any love. Don't think that your being lovable requires you to be prettier or smarter or cooler. You need to recognize all that you have to give to your spouse, or your religious vocation, or your chosen life. That good priest said love yourself and give that self away to someone who appreciates all that you are. Of course, his advice requires a good sense of self-esteem and real commitment. But it is a clear path that guides you in love. When you give your love, you want it to be accepted and appreciated. You do not want it to be dismissed or recognized only sometimes. You want someone who will sit with you, be present to you, and truly care for you. You want someone to take your hand. You want that big hug.

That advice helped me as I thought about what I wanted in life and as I wondered if I would ever find someone to whom I wanted to give the gift of myself. Marriage had been part of my plan since I was young. There was that time in first grade when I wanted to run a candy store, but that desire came more from my commitment to M&Ms than to a business. In second grade, I wanted to be a nun because I adored my teacher, who was a devoted nun. Back then I was enchanted because she let me dust her desk and she encouraged me to read. But, since third grade, I wanted to be a mother, a wife, and a writer.

I figured out how to do the writing. I started keeping journals in junior high and then worked on high school and college newspapers. However, the goals of a husband and children seemed to elude me. I dated but never could imagine walking down the aisle. My mother and her dear friends, my honorary aunts, would often say, in worried and hushed tones: "Our Peggy just might end up an old maid. She is too fussy." Fortunately, that term for a single woman is not used anymore, but as a young woman I knew what it meant: I would end up alone and unloved. I wouldn't even have a cat because I am allergic to them. I really wondered if anyone would appreciate me for me. Was there really someone out there who would love a woman who loved God, baseball, and chocolate and had little interest in fashion, decorating, or the great outdoors?

And then John came into my life. Four decades later, I still feel blessed that I found someone worthy of me. And I rejoice that he found someone worthy of him. The critical factor in this love formula is that the love is without qualification. John and our children know that I love them unconditionally. I do not say to my husband, "I love you but only if you bring me flowers or give me jewelry." I do not tell him that I love him only when he is in a good mood. Nor would I love him only if he were in good health. The vows were pretty clear: "I promise to be true to you in good times and in bad."

And once you decide that you found the right person to love, then you go all in. You just decide to love every day. Whether it is folding laundry, making meals, sitting through soccer practices, or fixing cars, you are all in. You are at eye level and giving your heart to the person or vocation or life that is worthy of you. Love is not glamorous or easy. But true love and devotion are amazing. Such love is the kind that brings spouses to nursing homes each day, even when the other spouse does not recognize them. Such love shines in the priest who goes to the hospital at 2 a.m. on a sick call. It radiates in the teacher who works on yet another strategy to help a student. Love is a mystery—but you know what it is when you see it. And you know how desperately we all need it.

A Hunger for Love

The desire to feel loved and valued and to feel that you belong is especially strong today, and even governments are recognizing this basic need for connection. The United Kingdom has gone so far as to appoint a "Minister for Loneliness." Prime Minister Theresa May made the appointment in January 2018. The *New York Times* reported that May said the position was necessary because loneliness is "a sad reality of modern life." The Minister for Loneliness focuses the department's efforts especially toward the elderly, caregivers, and those who have lost a loved one. The decision to create this department was based on government statistics that more than nine million people in the United Kingdom said they often or always felt lonely—a sizable percentage in a country with a total population of about sixty-six million. That number might be higher if you factor in people who did not want to admit how isolated or alone they really feel.

The government also reported that more than two hundred thousand older people said they had not had a conversation with a friend or relative in more than a month. Researchers also note that loneliness might be equated to smoking fifteen cigarettes a day in terms of the effect on health. Studies show that loneliness causes actual physical harm to people. The consequences of feeling unloved and isolated are significant.

Pope Francis understands the human condition and stresses that we must show our love. He said in a homily given in May 2018 at Santissimo Sacramento Parish in the outskirts of Rome: "Love is not what they say in movies. Love is not playing violins, all romantic. No, Love is work. Love shows itself in works, not in words."

The question each of us must ask is this: *Am I willing to do the work? Am I willing to visit the elderly aunt in a nursing home? Am I willing to listen to the story of a neighbor? Am I willing to listen to that same story several times?*

Or perhaps *you* need a listening ear. If so, are you willing to let people know that you're lonely? Love requires not only self-worth but also work and risk. Love can be comfortable and sweet, but it can take a great deal of effort. Hurts and sorrow and heartache can be intertwined with love, but all of us are worthy of love. And all of us can learn to show our love, if just by reaching out a hand to someone or by letting people simply be themselves as we sit beside them.

Saintly Inspiration

St. Pope John Paul II is a great example of someone who kept loving throughout his life. He could have been a sour, bitter person; his early life was filled with heartache. By the time he was twenty-one, he had lost his mother, his brother, and his father. The first Polish pope could have been afraid to love after all that misery and sadness. He could have been angry as he watched war rage in his country and people betrayed in so many ways. He could have not wanted to risk love again. After all, most of the people he had loved were gone, and the world was chaotic and violent. But St. Pope John Paul II did not give up. He chose to lead a life of love and service through the priesthood. God led him by the hand to his vocation. God told him to "sit, sit, sit" and be present with him. And St. Pope John Paul II used his priesthood and papacy to show his love for all—even the man who tried to assassinate him. He said, "Darkness can only be scattered by light and hatred can only be conquered by love." He never gave up on love.

That sense of being loved enough comes not from roses or jewelry or even attaining the title of pope. It comes while holding the hand of a dying person. It comes when writing a note to someone who is grieving. It comes when you give all your attention to another, whether that person is 2 years old, 22, or 102. Being loved and loving are not contradictory terms; they mean a balancing act of loving yourself enough, feeling loved enough, and loving others enough. This is a big challenge. It is a bit easier if you live out the Gospel call to love God with your whole heart and soul and to love your neighbor as yourself.

When in doubt, watch how little children love. They will show us the way.

Putting Faith into Practice

- Why send valentines only in February? Send a note of love to special people in your life. Then, send kind notes to people who may be struggling or lonely.

- Take an hour to make a date with a friend or your spouse or your child or your parent. No phones! No distractions. Just share an ice cream or a cup of tea and have a chat. Be present and listen.

- Take a moment. Sit in quiet. Think about what you like about yourself. Acknowledge you are not perfect but give yourself a pat on the back and say out loud, "I love you!"
- If possible, spend a little time with a child. It is astonishing how children's honesty and sincerity can help us see what love is all about.

Ignatian Examen

Give thanks.

Thank the Lord for all those who have loved you and made you feel valued. Continue this litany of gratitude and thank the Lord for all the people you have loved. Thank the Lord for yourself. And then thank the Lord for all he has created.

Ask for the Spirit.

Ask the good Lord to guide you as you discern your life and your loves. Seek his help as you determine how you want to live your life of love.

Review and recognize challenges and failures.

Have you been afraid to give your heart to others? Have you been afraid to truly love because of past hurts and feelings of inadequacy? Can you accept that God loves you? Have you hurt others?

Ask for forgiveness and healing.

Ask God to help you take someone's hand and show him or her love. Ask God to help you put aside hurts and believe in yourself and the love you can give and receive.

Pray about tomorrow.

Dear Lord, I know love is both beautiful and difficult. There are days when I do not love enough. And there are days when I do not feel loved enough. Help me see how important love is in my life and that it is worth the effort. Help me not give up on love. And thank you for all the love in my life.

5

Good Enough

Have patience with all things, but, first of all with yourself.
—St. Francis de Sales

You do not need to take notes for this chapter. Just scroll through your phone or flip through your television channels or scan the pages of a magazine. How are families portrayed? From these sources, what would you conclude is a perfect family? Okay, maybe not perfect, but an ideal family? What does it look like? Do those images or ideas inspire you? Here's hoping you will figure out that you and yours are who you are and that God made you in his image and likeness.

Loving Your Family

Every family is unique. We know that, but we often feel that ours is just a little too unique and possibly not quite *enough*. We might have a few misgivings about our family—either the one in which we were raised or the one we might be raising or have raised. Families can be complicated and difficult and hard to navigate. And it's quite natural to look around at other families and think that yours is maybe not as accomplished or close or well-functioning as the ones you see around you. It's easy to think, *My family is not like other families.* And then it is easy for questions to creep in and for you to measure your family by the various images of family that you see. You wonder if you and your loved ones are okay. You wonder if you are a good enough parent, spouse, sibling, or child. You think, *I bet that family doesn't fight over who ate the last cupcake or whose turn it is to unload the dishwasher or sit in the front seat of the car.* Or you truly bare your soul and think, *I bet that family is better at dealing with a rebellious teenager or a depressed spouse. I bet they're not facing addiction or divorce.*

But all this looking and wondering and comparing yourself to others can wear on you. It can make it difficult to see God's beautiful creation all around us. It can make it difficult to see, as St. Ignatius of Loyola put it, God in all things.

St. Matthew's Gospel hammers the message home even more: "For where two or three are gathered together in my name, I am there in the midst of them" (Matthew 18:20).

It would be so nice to always have the clarity to see the good in others and Christ's presence among them. Yet how easy it is to compare our own situation with others' instead. We are told we should see Jesus in everyone. We are taught we should see others as part of our wider family. And we want to see our own family as a group that is not perfect but at least offers a spot where one is loved and accepted. But this can be a real struggle.

You look at those near you, but you do not always see them as your beloved brothers and sisters. You probably do not look at them with disdain, but you do look with the frantic eyes of insecurity. You notice. You notice your neighbor's new car. You notice where people go on vacation. You notice whose child is on the school honor roll or the all-star team. You notice if your child is the only one crying in church. You notice who is included on a committee and who is not. You notice how your family shapes up next to others.

It happens even at places where one should find solace and peace. It has happened to me in church. Instead of piously bowing my head in prayer before or after communion, I often watch the people walking in the communion line. Sometimes what I notice is encouraging, and it is heartening to see a dear parishioner make his or her way up the aisle. However, many times, I notice what people wear or how they look or whether they're singing or how they're walking. Then I realize that I've begun to judge others as well as myself.

As a young parent, I was particularly aware of other families. I remember one such experience as I sat in church on a Sunday morning with my family. There had been the usual rush and the "hurry-up-we're-going-to-be-late-for-Mass" moments. We weren't in our Sunday best, but I was grateful we got out the door in time. As I looked around, I noticed a family that looked like they had just stepped out of a fashion catalog. Each child wore a crisply ironed outfit. The girls had fancy braids in their hair. The parents looked polished and put together. They looked lovely. I should have been praying and thanking God for my wonderful family—because I do love them to bits. And I should have been celebrating and admiring the family that was dressed so nicely. Instead, I was watching and comparing and worrying.

On that particular Sunday morning, a part of me did not feel like a good-enough parent. Watching the other family made me think of all the things I was not. I have never cared about fashion and do not like ironing, but I measured myself next to the wrinkle-free, perfectly coiffed family and felt inadequate. It sounds silly now. But we need to address those feelings of inadequacy if we're going to deal adequately with our feeling not good enough. On that Sunday, I wondered, *How does that mom manage to get all of those kids looking so spiffy for church?* Most days it was a challenge for me to get the laundry out of the dryer without too many wrinkles. My best effort at hairstyling was to hire a local teenager to do a French braid in my daughter's hair when she was a junior bridesmaid in a wedding. When my family went to church, my children did not look like children in a Charles Dickens novel, but neither did they look like the starched and super-braided family I had witnessed that Sunday. Today, I can laugh at myself. Back then, I wondered if I was a good enough mother. I compared myself to other moms who just seemed to have everything together. I believed that other families were perfect and had not bickered all the way to church about important issues like donuts or the comics section or who was breathing on whom.

Comparing Yourself

Comparing, wondering, and worrying. We fall into those patterns for so many reasons. Kids do it in school. They receive their graded test papers and buzz with the question, "What did you get?" Adults ask one another how much they paid for this or that. Or, where did they go on vacation? What extracurricular activities are their children involved with? Proud parents offer, unsolicited, the latest news about which universities accepted their high school graduates. Whether we ask the questions or are offered the information, we tend to measure our lives and our children's lives by what is happening in other families.

As a parent I tried to brush those insecurities aside, but parenthood can also bring them right back in a heartbeat. Family life is wonderful and hard. It is a joy to bring a little one into the world. It also introduces worries, doubts, and fears. Breast or bottle? Work or stay home? Should you have played classical music when the baby was in the womb instead of listening to rock music? Why do people have such strong opinions about pacifiers? And then the watching of the baby begins. The very nature of how they are measured invites comparison; you might fret over whether your child is in the 5th or 95th percentile in height or weight.

It should get easier as you grow in confidence as a parent, but often it doesn't. This is especially true for first-time parents. You wonder when your baby will walk, talk, or read. You wonder if you are good enough and doing enough. And you think that somehow everyone is doing it better as you watch another child reach a milestone before your child does. I would often tell my children that it is important to rejoice in the success or good fortune of others. But I did not always listen to my own advice.

Addressing those feelings of insecurity is necessary if you want to embrace the truth that you are good enough. You have to figure out who you are and then love who you are. Part of my reaction to worrying about being a good enough parent was to say, "Get over yourself. Everyone is fine, and focus on what matters." But another part of me allowed the seeds of doubt to take root, and this sometimes meant that I focused on the wrong things.

For example, our parish asked the children making their first communion to create a banner for each pew. My eight-year-old daughter was better at art than I was—actually, she had been better than I was since she was just five years old. But I worried that our banner, which would be on display at the end of our pew and was meant to honor this important day, wouldn't be good enough artistically. Instead of enjoying this special moment, I was worried about a hot-glue gun and pieces of felt. On Kerry's big day, I looked around and noticed that other parents had helped create gorgeous banners with glitter, jewels, vines, and intricate chalices. Kerry's was fine. She liked it and still has it. However, I remember wishing that I had been an artsy mom who could have pitched in some creativity and glitter.

Another time, my son, Matthew, came home from first grade and said, "Andrew told me that he is going to be a lion for Halloween. And he said his mom is going to sew his costume. Did you know that moms could sew Halloween costumes?" His astonishment was priceless, and he seemed content when I told him that I knew some moms could make costumes but that he had gotten a reading mom, not a sewing mom. Matthew seemed satisfied with the answer, but I realized that buying Batman pajamas and safety-pinning a blue pillowcase to them to make a cape was not going to win a costume prize. Still, we did it. And now I know that such Halloween costumes will not ruin a child for life. But there are days when you are so unsure, so uncertain.

And one does not have to be raising children to feel this insecurity. It can be prompted by any sort of family. You might look around and wish you came from a bigger or smaller family. You might wish your parents or siblings were quieter or more outgoing. And you might even think that every other family has fewer problems and that they have a Thanksgiving dinner that looks like the iconic portrait painted by Norman Rockwell. The glasses and china are shimmering. The turkey is cooked perfectly, and everyone is smiling and happy.

You might even try to emulate those ideals. I certainly have. One of my family's favorite meals is pot roast with carrots, mashed potatoes, and gravy. I've made this meal many times, but one is particularly memorable for us. We had just gathered around the table, and I felt quite pleased, maybe even a bit smug. After all, it was a summer night, but I had sweated and worked hard to gather everyone for this culinary palate pleaser.

Now, I need to confess that the potatoes were homemade, but the gravy came from a mix. I have never mastered my mother's talent for making great gravy, so mine comes from water and a packet. We all sat down and piled the food on our plates. My husband and son splashed gravy on everything and dug in.

Matthew was the first to comment that the gravy tasted funny. My husband sniffed his plate and added that the gravy also smelled funny. My daughters seemed glad that they had not gotten the gravy first. I looked around the table and told them they were all ridiculous. After all, how can you mess up packaged gravy? I grabbed the empty packets out of the trash. Was there an expiration date on them? Did I buy strangely flavored gravy? No and no.

I flipped through the packages to spot any irregularities. Finally, I flipped to the last packet, which read "Taco Mix." At last we knew why the gravy tasted strange. I felt deflated and disappointed. Our big family meal was awash in strange tastes and ruined food. I was not Betty Crocker! But then everyone just started laughing. To this day, the "taco gravy" story has become something we chuckle about every time I pull out those paper packets to make gravy—of course, now I double-check them. Mistakes are part of family life. And I suspect that every family has a funny failure story to tell, but I would never know that from observing from the outside. So, not only am I comparing my family experience to the experiences of other families, but I am also comparing my family experience to *my imagined experiences* of other families.

Always Comparing

It can be hard to watch and listen and not compare. Years ago, I was standing with some moms as we waited to pick up our children from their kindergarten class. I held the hand of our four-year-old; I was also pregnant with our third child. If anyone had an excuse to neglect housework, it was me. But another mother, in all earnestness, told me that she had a housework system. She said she cleaned two rooms thoroughly each day and was able to keep up with the dirt and mess. I listened, knowing my beds were not made and there were Teenage Mutant Ninja Turtles figures all over our family-room floor. I told her that her system sounded very good. I did not add that I knew I could not do it. Honestly, I knew I *would* not. But I was a new mom at the school, so I just smiled. And I wondered why I did not care about those things. I wondered if I was a good enough homemaker.

I wondered if my children would ever stop saying, "Who is coming over?" whenever they saw me cleaning.

Years later, I listened to another mom who was standing outside the school waiting to pick up her daughter. I was there for my youngest. This mom said she had begun preparations for her Christmas-cookie baking. It took her a month to do it all. She was proud and excited. This time, I praised her for her efforts but did not remain silent. I added that I just usually bought the slice-and-bake sugar cookies and let the kids decorate them. There were other moms there listening. I hope they realized that their worth was not dependent upon their creativity during the holiday season, that they were good enough no matter what kind of cookie making or buying they chose. It can be hard.

One year my youngest child was on a soccer team. Each week, parents were asked to bring a snack for the team. The coach suggested orange slices and crackers. Each week, I watched as parents went above and beyond in a new sport: competitive snack making. There were goodie bags, decorated cupcakes, fruit kebabs, and cookies decorated like soccer balls. Goodness, do I dare bring orange slices and Goldfish crackers? This time, I did not. I joined the competitive line and brought homemade cookies and little fruit cups. I wanted my snack to be good enough. I wanted to be seen as a good-enough parent. And I wanted my child to think I had done enough. I am sure that child does not remember the soccer snack. But I do because it was one more time when I allowed other people's actions to influence how I valued myself.

You may also have tales of fretting and comparing and wondering if you and your family are enough. Questions and worries may bombard you, especially concerning your children and especially when more serious questions like death, divorce, or other difficult times are involved. Do you feel like a lesser family? Do you feel broken? Can you just be glad to be a reading person instead of a sewing person? Can you celebrate who you are instead of being someone else?

Even though my children are grown, I still worry about whether our family is good enough. However, I have, for the most part, set aside those feelings of inadequacy. I have turned to rejoicing in what I see others do instead of comparing my own actions to them. It is important to realize that the key is not to stop watching but to rejoice in what you see. Pope Francis brings comfort and inspiration: "We should not be fearful of imperfections, weakness, or even conflict, but rather learn how to deal with them constructively. The family, where we keep loving one another despite our limits and sins, thus becomes a school of forgiveness."

A Place of Acceptance

These words of the Holy Father should help us see that one's home should be a place of acceptance. For when you truly love one another, you understand that you will make mistakes and annoy people and disappoint them and yourself. However, you also will find a place of comfort and solace and deep affection. If you can extend that notion of family to a parish or a neighborhood or a community, then it might be possible to become more accepting of others and learn to love one another and support one another. It would be great if we could help families and communities become places where more love abounds and fretful comparisons wither.

Being part of a family involves openness and trust that help people feel accepted. It is critical to stop watching, comparing, and worrying and begin plain-old loving. True love will mean that you are cherished as you are, by God and others. You will receive the message that you are good enough. No one says to a baby, "I love you, but I wish you could pick up after yourself." No one looks at a two-year-old and says, "You are great, but you should be reading." You just love them and nurture them and hug them and hope for the best for them. Extend that feeling to yourself and your world. It can be hard, probably hardest, when you try and pat yourself on the back and say, "There, there. You are fine just the way you are." But try it anyway.

Saintly Inspiration

A good lesson in making people feel good enough comes from a woman who was called Mother by millions but had no children of her own. St. Mother Teresa of Calcutta was born in 1910 and lived a good life as a nun and teacher. Then she received what she described as "a call within a call." She went on to found the Missionaries of Charity, to help the poorest of the poor. She died in 1997 and was canonized in 2016. Hers sounds like an ideal and saintly life, but Mother Teresa also led a truly difficult life as she struggled with her faith and her relationship with God. Her writings reveal her worries. In a 2007 book by Brian Kolodiejchuk, her letters show how hard it was for her: "Where is my faith? Even deep down . . . there is nothing but emptiness and darkness. . . . If there be God—please forgive me. When I try to raise my thoughts to Heaven, there is such convicting emptiness that those very thoughts return like sharp knives and hurt my very soul."

Imagine this holy woman going around and giving speeches and encouraging her fellow nuns while feeling this way. Imagine how often she must not have felt good enough, worthy enough. But she stuck it out through prayer, persistence, and the grace of God.

And that is how you can realize you are good enough. You can know that a saint felt terrible but kept believing. God made the world and saw that it was good—more than good enough. And that world includes you.

Putting Faith into Practice

- Look around where you are and appreciate all that you see. If a bedroom is messy, be glad you have a bed. If a closet is disorganized, be glad you have clothes. And if you or your family seem wanting—well, be glad you have those people in your life.

- Watch television shows and advertisements and see how *family* is portrayed. Ask yourself how that compares to your own family. Then identify what is true and untrue about the fictional depictions.

- Finish this sentence:

  Family is . . .

  This will help you sort out some of your feelings about what you desire for your family. It can also give you the opportunity to say to yourself that you and your family are already loved by God, accepted as you are—good enough.

Ignatian Examen

Give thanks.

Thank the Lord for the skills you have. Rejoice that you have a green thumb. Be happy if you are artistic. And do not mind if the only thing you can draw is a bath. And thank God for the family you have. It is yours and helped form you into the good person you are.

Ask for the Spirit.

Ask the good Lord for the ability to resist getting caught up in constantly comparing yourself or your family to others. Ask for the peace of mind that comes from enjoying your own family situation, however frazzled or fractured it may be.

Review and recognize challenges and failures.

When are you tempted to worry about what others are doing or about what others think? How can you make a practice of rejoicing in the success and happiness of others?

Ask for forgiveness and healing.

Ask God to help you see the good in yourself and those around you. Make a commitment to forgive those in your family who have hurt you (sometimes this can take a while, so be patient but persistent). Cherish your children for their own unique selves. And cherish yourself.

Pray about tomorrow.

Try this prayer: *Dear Lord, give me the peace of mind to work toward contentment. Guide me as I look at my family and myself and see them as truly being good enough. Help me rid my mind of notions of perfection and help me to focus on love.*

6
Stuff Enough

*Our possessions are not ours—God has given them to us to
cultivate, that we may make them fruitful and profitable in His
Service, and so doing we shall please Him.*
—St. Francis de Sales

Whenever I buy a lottery ticket, I ask myself what I would do if I
won a million dollars. What would you do with a million dollars? Go
ahead, make a list. Then make another list of what you really need.
Do they match? Probably not. Wants and needs are different. And
figuring out what you really need is the beginning of understanding
when you have stuff enough.

How Much Is Too Much?

It is reported that the average woman owns seven purses. I confess
that I like purses, so that number is higher in my closet. However, I
just read about a celebrity who had a purse room in her house. She
devoted an entire room just to hold her purses. Another article told
of a woman who has a collection of more than 200 bags worth $1.8
million. Perhaps one of them was an Hermès Birkin purse, with dia-
monds, which recently sold for $380,000.

It is easy to sit back in righteous indignation and look at people
who have such excess in their lives. You think that they are greedy,
materialistic persons. You can take the moral high ground and be like

the Pharisee in Luke's Gospel and say, "O God, I thank you that I am not like the rest of humanity." You can think, "O God, I am glad I am not like the celebrity with all those purses. I would never amass cars in such great numbers and at such an expense." But then you have to look in the mirror. Or maybe take a peek in your own closet or garage. Then ask some questions.

What is excess? How much is too much? How much stuff is enough?

The Value of Stuff

Recently, I have read articles that warn people to clean out their closets and pare down their things because their heirs are not going to want any of it. One headline read, "No one wants your stuff." Yet every Black Friday and Cyber Monday, we are encouraged to spend, spend, spend and buy more stuff for ourselves and others.

I invite you to look around your home and think about what you have.

As I write these words, on my dresser I see a Waterford crystal baseball that has the name of my favorite team (the Boston Red Sox) etched into it. My children and husband gave it to me for my birthday and as a reminder of our visit to the Baseball Hall of Fame in Cooperstown, New York. That ball is a treasure to me. It represents many things I love: family, baseball, my Irish heritage, and beauty—all in one small item. Yet some might see that ball as excess. Others might think it is silly to purchase a ball that collects dust and can never be thrown. However, when thinking about our belongings and asking how much is enough, it seems wise to consider beauty and personal value. When I consider what this ball means to me, I recognize that material things are not bad in themselves. Rather, the problem seems to lie in the need for more and the endless cycle of acquisition.

I struggle to find a balance. How much is too much? And what does any person really need?

Think about the families who have experienced natural disasters. Imagine the many wildfires that have raged through California, burning homes to the ground. People had only a few hours' notice to pack what mattered and flee. Consider the devastation of floods experienced in other parts of the country. With sometimes just moments to spare, people are forced to jump into boats and flee with only the clothes on their backs. In news segment after news segment, people who have experienced these disasters express gratitude about being alive. They say that things can be replaced—"It's just stuff." But they acknowledge that treasured items, photographs, and keepsakes that matter are all gone now. You learn from watching these survivors that not all stuff is bad. It is good to have clean sheets, dishes, pans, and clothes.

I have wondered what I would take with me if forced to leave my home on short notice. What would I pack if I just had a few minutes' warning? What would you pack? Are you surprised by your answers? At the moment of crisis, you have more clarity about what matters. We love getting gifts and buying new things. But when we are ill or facing family problems, we recognize that a new sweater, or even a nicer car, does not matter that much.

When I consider what I would pack in a crisis, I list those things I could never replace. If I had enough time, I would want to pack the christening gown that has been worn by my three children and many grandchildren. Old photos I meant to scan into digital files would be next. Jewelry that was handed down the generations or received on special occasions would go into the bag. Then I would pack the old tin sifter that sits on my kitchen counter. It depicts a woman wearing a big apron, and she has two little children at her side as she prepares to bake. It was my mother's and is a symbol to me of her love of cooking and her even greater love of family. It is too old to use for sifting, but this gadget from the 1940s represents my mom's sense of hospitality. She tried to feed anyone who came in her door and was the first to send a meal when someone was having a tough time. So the impractical sifter goes in the bag. And, yes, I would take the Waterford crystal baseball, if I had the time and room. And if I had more time, I would pack the green, blue, and gold sparkly bulldog that my son painted for me years ago. I also would pick up the file of artwork made by my children. And while I am in the file cabinet, it would probably be wise to get the folder with birth certificates and other legal documents.

Your list is unique to your life, memories, and priorities. The point is not to compare our lists but to understand what we value and why. To give ourselves permission to value the things that matter and to let go of those that don't.

Taking Stock

The key question "How much is enough?" is not easy to answer. Sure, most would agree that owning enough purses to fill their own room is excessive. But what is the cutoff? There are those who lobby the Vatican to sell off its artwork and other treasures to help the poor. Would this solve the world's problems in a lasting, systemic way? Or is there inherent value in art and beauty? Many see the beauty of art or a church or a stained-glass window as a way to spread the word of God so that hearts and minds can be transformed.

Make your own list of your most precious possessions, the ones you'd take with you if a fire were approaching. Study your list. When I look at the list I just made, I know that I would be sad if I lost these items, but I would be okay. It would be a horrible experience but nothing compared to the loss of a loved one. Even though I like my stuff, I would survive without it. And you would think that after realizing this fact, I would vow to shop less. However, I know that I will not stop shopping because I still want to buy things for my husband, my children, my grandchildren, my home, and, yes, myself. Perhaps the questions you might ask yourself are: Why do I feel the need to acquire nonessential things? What does surrounding myself with stuff do for me? What does this need really mean? Do I own my possessions or do my possessions own me? Do I feel the need to have the "right" clothes or car so others will see me as important and valuable? Do I feel powerful when I purchase and gather—and is that feeling sustaining or fleeting? Do I keep buying things to feed a hunger that will never be filled by clothes, purses, jewelry, or gadgets? Do I think that the only way to make my loved ones appreciate me is to buy things for them?

There is so much to consider.

More than twenty years ago, I was helping out in the lunchroom at my children's school. Women were chatting about their Christmas shopping. The hunt was on for the items on the Santa list. One mom said she spent about $1,000 on each of her three children—with inflation, that's $4,800 in today's dollars. That comment stayed with me because I found that amount staggering. The desire to show her children how much she loved them was real, but the amount spent seemed unreal. Another mom told me that she and her husband borrowed from his retirement fund to take their children to Disney World. Now, there is nothing wrong with Mickey's kingdom, but many families believe they *must* go to the "happiest place on earth" no matter what the cost.

It is easy to feel that we're above such excesses. It can be easy to feel that I live simply and humbly compared to others. But then the words of Pope Francis resonate: "Who am I to judge?" And I take a hard look at myself and think back to the many times I have prized material goods.

In 1984, there was a phenomenon that seems silly now: the Cabbage Patch Kid craze. Everyone wanted these homely little dolls with yarn hair, plastic heads, and each with a unique birth certificate. They were cute in a funny kind of way. Still, the response to these dolls was unbelievable. News reports showed shoppers camping out overnight at toy stores to get them. Others stormed the displays that had them, triggering fights and riot conditions in some places. *Merry Christmas, I bring you tidings of great joy and peace—now get out of my way so I can get a doll to make my child happy!*

At the time, I was not too caught up in the craze. My daughter Kerry was just two, and her little brother, Matthew, was barely one. What need did my children have for this sought-after toy? But then the phone call came. Our family was in Milwaukee, visiting family for Thanksgiving. We had made a special effort to travel during this busy holiday because my husband's father had been diagnosed with cancer. Our focus was on this good and loving family man. Still, amid the sadness I heard the siren song of the Cabbage Patch Kid doll.

My sister-in-law told me that she had gotten word from her sister-in-law that the store where she worked was getting a shipment of Cabbage Patch Kid dolls and she could get us some if we came right away. My sister-in-law and I both jumped at the chance to get these must-have dolls. Like two spies on a mission, we ran to the car to drive forty-five minutes to the store. We were told that we had to act quickly and quietly because the dolls were going to be put on the shelves soon and would not last long. We met the sister-in-law of my sister-in-law near the back of the store. She handed us wrapped packages. Each contained two dolls. We had hit the jackpot. We clutched them as if we had been given a great prize. We had gotten the hot toy! We put them in the car and drove home. We laugh about the incident today, but at the time we were thrilled.

A few days later, my husband and I flew home with our children, ages one and two. I was reluctant to put the dolls in our suitcase for fear that they would be taken. So I carried them onto the plane—boarding with two children, a diaper bag, and my purse. I don't remember but hope I did not make Kerry walk so I could carry the dolls. They were wrapped tightly and stowed safely in the overhead compartment. The flight attendant asked what was in the packages. Feeling proud and a little smug, I told her. She gave me a big smile and told me I was one of the fortunate ones. It is embarrassing to say this now, but I kept an eye on those dolls while we were on the plane, and I breathed a sigh of relief when I got them home. One of the dolls went to my three-year-old niece who lived nearby. The other was our "big" Christmas gift for Kerry.

On Christmas morning, my two-year-old opened the present. She looked at the doll and seemed to like it, but she didn't care that much about it. Why would she? She had no idea it was *the* toy to have. She seemed just as happy with her other gifts. And, like most little ones, she had more fun with the boxes and wrapping paper. It was a true epiphany for me. I had been so very silly, listening to the voices telling me that a certain toy would make a child happier or a holiday more special. To this day, the doll reminds me not to get too caught up in trends and must-haves. Kerry still has the doll in her closet at home. She knows the story of how it got there. It is a source of amusement. But, for me, it's also a strong symbol of how acquiring an object can become more than just a purchase. You think, "Once I get a new car, I will be content." Or you believe, "It's worth maxing out my credit card to take a trip or put a smile on my loved one's face." That year, I thought that giving my daughter the doll would make her happy and I would be a better parent because she got the toy of the year.

What Is Essential

Christmas is probably the holiday on which people feel the most pressure about material things. Recently, I read a letter on Facebook that was shared more than 150,000 times. It was from a dying woman who asked her family not to buy presents for one another but to write meaningful cards to one another instead. She said the holiday was special and stress-free. She died just ten days after Christmas. This young woman's perspective certainly had been changed by the knowledge that she would be leaving this world, yet the advice resonates. It echoes the words from Dr. Seuss's *How the Grinch Stole Christmas*. The heartwarming book teaches us that joy does not come from possessions. Even after the Grinch stole all the presents in town, the families were able to celebrate this special time, happily. The Grinch figured out that Christmas "doesn't come from a store."

Still, you want stuff. You want to shop. You want to give tangible gifts to others. And you get caught up in it. You listen to the call to buy, buy, buy. For instance, you look around and see toddlers with electronic tablets. The call for new technologies is relentless, with empty promises of more "connectivity" and efficiencies and safety. If you pay even a little attention to the shouts of advertising, you may be convinced that you cannot exist without gadgets such as "the best" wireless headphones, a Bluetooth speaker, a portable smartphone charger, a handheld camera, a GoPro camera, a selfie stick, and a fitness tracker. Do these items really make your life better or easier? What helps you connect with the people you love?

Give Me Only Your Love and Grace

Even during times when we should be most focused on the people in front of us, we are bombarded with voices telling us to spend. This has become especially prominent when it comes to weddings. It is your special day—will it be any less special if you do not have your monogram carved in ice? A recent poll by The Knot asked thirteen thousand recently married couples how much they paid for their wedding. The average cost was more than $35,000. The costs varied by region, but the wedding industry keeps driving home the message: This is your day! Spend!

I'm not trying to make anyone feel guilty. But it's good for any of us, from time to time, to reassess what we do and why, what we value and why, what we spend and why.

United Nations statistics reveal that nearly half of the world's population—more than three billion people—live on less than $2.50 a day. More than 805 million people worldwide do not have enough food to eat. It's reasonable to ask ourselves if our spending is justified; how much is enough? While you and I are brushing our teeth, more than 750 million people lack adequate access to clean drinking water. And when we flip off our lights tonight, one-quarter of all humans will be living without electricity.

As I let these figures sink in, I imagine myself at the pearly gates. St. Peter is greeting me but also grilling me: "Were you aware that so many of your brothers and sisters went to bed hungry while you upgraded your phone?" Yes. "And you did this because you needed more memory to take pictures while others just needed a meal every day?" "Um, yes," I would say again as I looked at my feet. There really is no good explanation for some of the actions we decide to take. Or is there? And so I struggle. We all struggle, no matter the size of our bank account or house. Part of our shared journey is to figure out the right balance in life and decide what is enough and what we really need.

Saintly Inspiration

St. Ignatius of Loyola, founder of the Jesuits, underwent an amazing conversion experience and, to serve Jesus, he gave up his military r, his worldly goods, and his aspirations for fame and fortune. He began his religious life by begging and praying. It is no wonder that his Suscipe prayer provides so much inspiration and guidance. He gave up all he had to follow Christ. I wonder what I am willing to give up.

> Take, Lord, and receive all my liberty,
> my memory, my understanding,
> and my entire will,
> All I have and call my own.
>
> You have given all to me.
> To you, Lord, I return it.
>
> Everything is yours; do with it what you will.
> Give me only your love and your grace,
> that is enough for me.
>
> —St. Ignatius of Loyola

Putting Faith into Practice

Try these ideas to rid yourself of the need to gather nonessential stuff.

- Look through your closet or another area of your home and choose what to keep and what to give away or throw away.
- Put a sticky note on your wallet that will make you pause as you pull out a credit card to make another purchase.
- Give up shopping for anything besides food for this week or for Lent or Advent.

Ignatian Examen

Give thanks.

Thank the Lord for what you have. Conduct a mental inventory of your blessings, physical or material, one by one.

Ask for the Spirit.

Ask God, *How much is enough for me?* Resist wallowing in guilt; pray for the guidance to recognize what truly matters to you. Consider that the Lord's love and grace might be enough for you.

Review and recognize challenges and failures.

Have you wasted time or money on material things? What might you have collected that is excessive or unnecessary? When do you care too much about what people think of you or your possessions? When do you feel the need to have the "right" stuff? Do you ever think that others will like you more if you keep giving possessions rather than personal connection? Take some time to think about these things now.

Ask for forgiveness and healing.

Ask God to help you shed the need for stuff. Request the grace to recognize that if all your things went away tomorrow, you would still be you, a child of God who is loved.

Pray about tomorrow.

Try this prayer: *Dear Lord, help me face tomorrow with an open and generous heart. Help me see that I can give myself to others in so many ways. Guide me to write a note or make a phone call or bake a cookie for someone else. Or just let this prayer be my gift today, to myself and others.*

Repeat the words of St. Ignatius: *Give me only your love and grace—that's enough for me.*

7
Impressive Enough

Humility consists in not esteeming ourselves above other men, and
in not seeking to be esteemed above them.
—St. Francis de Sales

Write your name on paper or type it into your computer, tablet, or phone. Think of this as your "business card." What do you list beneath your name? Educator? Parent? Baseball fan? Chocolate lover? Engineer? Part-time singer? Artist? Aspiring saint? Who we are, and who others think we are, matters, like it or not. Get ready to explore how you feel about how you impress others.

Wanting to Impress

When I was a child, I lived in a world that was enough for me. There was no one I really wanted to impress. I didn't give a thought to where I lived; home was home. It was a close-knit world for me because I lived across the street from my church and my school. Nobody in our neighborhood traveled much, and we all could walk to the nearby park and library. Our family shopped at a grocery store that I now realize was just a small market. I had two or three dresses, some play clothes, and a few books. I didn't notice or think about the square footage or the décor of my home.

Our houses were close enough to each other that I could hear our neighbor's dryer buzz when the clothes were dry, and our neighbor on the other side would request an encore of a song when my brother practiced his accordion. Home was a place where I felt loved. I was happy. My world was small, and it was easy to remain oblivious to what others were doing. But when I was about nine, I probably had my first thought about wanting to impress others.

It was summertime and some kids in the neighborhood had gone to the New York World's Fair. Very few of us had ventured out of New England, so the idea of going from Massachusetts all the way to Queens, New York, was remarkable. I did not quite understand what a World's Fair was, but I knew that when the kids in my neighborhood returned from it, many of them were wearing a fancy felt hat that had their name sewn on it and—the best part—a large feather jutting out from the side. Today I can see that the hat was kind of goofy, but I must admit that back then I really wanted one of those jaunty caps. I didn't really yearn to go to the World's Fair or to endure a long car ride to get there. I just wanted that hat and the pleasure of walking around my street with it on my head: I wanted to be like the other kids. That was my first feeling of wanting to fit in and be accepted and to impress and the beginning of my awareness of what others thought of me—or what I assumed they thought of me.

Yet, I knew that this really fantastic hat was not in my future. Our family did not go on big trips, so I figured I would not ever get to impress anyone on Alderman Street with this sought-after souvenir. Then, to my great surprise, I learned that my family was going to go to the New York World's Fair. I was shocked and delighted and wondered how this happened. And then I realized that we made the four-hour car ride for only one reason: God. Truly, the only thing that could get my mother to go on this momentous trip was God. Oh, the Creator did not speak to her directly and say, "Connie, take your family to the World's Fair." But my mother knew that Michelangelo's *Pietà* was on display at the fair. It had been sent from the Vatican to

New York, and people were flocking to see the beautiful sculpture. My mother probably thought that she would never get to Italy (she never did) to see the famous statue of her beloved Blessed Mother holding the crucified Jesus in her arms. So we piled into our green Dodge, with no seatbelts, and definitely no cell phone app to guide us, and headed south.

I remember three things about that day at the fair. I recall my mother's face as she stood and stared at the beautiful *Pietà* sculpture. I knew the work of art was significant, but I didn't really appreciate it until I was older. But my mother, being a good friend of the Blessed Mother, was in awe of and absolutely touched by this work of art. My mom prayed her rosary daily and seemed to understand this depiction of the sorrowful mother. I also remember that we got to go on a ride called "It's a Small World," which I thought was wonderful. Little did I know that I would be riding on it again with my children at Disney World many years later. And, most important for me, I remember my parents letting me get the coveted feathered hat. I returned to my street and walked around with it on my head for a few days. I loved that hat, and I wanted everyone to see that I had been to the World's Fair too. That hat told everyone that I, too, was part of the crowd that got to go. Later, the hat just became a dust catcher on my dresser, and then it ended up in my closet and ultimately the trash bin. But it sat in my room for a long time as a true status symbol.

What is your first memory of wanting the status of fitting in? Did you think that a certain outfit would make you popular and create loads of friends? Or did you think kids in class would like you if you bought them candy or acted silly? Did you think you had to drink or drive a cool car to make a splash? Did you think you would be impressive enough if you got good grades or became a cheerleader or got elected as a class officer? Maybe you can recall your own "feathered hat" that you thought would impress others. Somehow, you often think those titles or that status will make you enough. A part of you tries to convince yourself that people will like you just for you. You can sing Mister Rogers' song lyrics: "It's you I like, every part of you." You can say you believe it. But, too often, there is another voice inside whispering that you are not impressive enough. There is a part of you that hungers for validation and reassurance.

Effects of Social Media

One way many of us look for that human connection and reassurance today is through social media. In this digital age, most people have some kind of account that connects them to others. It can be fun and encouraging as people "like" what you do. But sometimes it is overwhelming and makes it appear that many of your "friends" or followers are having a much better and more impressive life than yours. It can feel as if you're getting a "look at our great life" Christmas newsletter every day. It can feel as if everyone has a feathered hat except you.

In my experience, few people post their mishaps or problems on Facebook. Some share their sorrows, but most put up photos of their fabulous vacation or the great show they just saw. I have done it. If I am at opening day at Fenway Park, I share it. I am thrilled to be there and want everyone to know that I am enjoying a great day with my son. I see social media as informative. I enjoy looking at the photos and articles my friends and family members post, and I have learned a lot through articles and videos I've seen through social media.

I also know that I had a good time at an event, regardless of how many "likes" I get. And lately, a lot of my life has revolved around my grandchildren, and our family limits postings about them, so my contact with the cyberworld is not that strong. An advantage of getting older is that, more often than not, I no longer feel pressure to impress people. Yet it can be more difficult for children or teens or young adults to cope with the pressures of social media. A recent Pew survey showed that 92 percent of teens go online daily. Most of them do so using a mobile device. Teens and many other people are looking at their phones many, many times a day. Reports have shown that there has been a rise in sleeplessness, worry, and loneliness among teenagers who use their cell phones excessively. Another study, by psychologist Jean Twenge, found that many teens who spend five hours per day on an electronic device have at least one suicide risk factor. We've heard anecdotes, too, of teens being reduced to tears by the constant communication and comparisons that social media invites. Research tells us that girls, especially, say they feel pressured to live a "perfect" online life, and a large proportion of young women say they experience negative emotions while using the Internet. When I was a kid, you might have heard about a party and wished you had been invited to it, but you did not have to look at pictures of it online and see all the smiling people having a great time. Or maybe you knew people were going to a dance or concert, but you did not have to watch a video of everyone laughing and singing—everyone, it seems, but you. But now the world follows teens everywhere, and every day they see something that they are missing or not a part of.

Many are tempted constantly to measure themselves by the whims of clicks or swipes. They want to go viral or be affirmed by their peers but fear they will not. They look at their phones multiple times a day to see how they're doing in cyberspace. They even compare what kinds of phones they have and who has the latest and fastest model. They live in a viral world—and so do a lot of adults.

Pope Francis said he notices how enmeshed young people are in a virtual world of cell phones and other technology. "We have to make young people 'land' in the real world. Touch reality. Without destroying the good things the virtual world can have," he said in an address on May 14, 2018.

Although we might be advised to simply avoid social media—and make our children do the same—the fact remains that social media provide multiple means of connection. A young person who is denied that access might experience isolation in a different way. Also, we don't want to disregard the value of new technology. I love using Face-Time to talk with my grandchildren on my phone. It is wonderful to see their faces and hear their voices. I've even read stories and sung to them via technology. I love looking at photos of faraway family members via social media. And I learn so much through the virtual world. But we have to remember that our lives are so much more complicated and so much richer than what can be conveyed on a screen.

Everyone Matters

We should always try to avoid making judgments about a social media post or even a quick meeting with someone. We must not reduce the lives of the people we meet to only what we can see. Have you ever described someone as "just a ____." Or described yourself as "just a ____." I have heard so many women say, "I'm just a mom." They might not think that title is a big deal, but it truly is a life-changing vocation. I have heard waiters or waitresses say they are "just a server," yet they are much more than that, and their kindness or care can change a meal or a person's dining experience. When you go out to eat with a small child or an elderly person and the server is patient and pleasant, that means something.

It's important to remember that every person matters regardless of what his or her job is. There was a man who sold tickets every time we entered a local park. He greeted everyone with a smile and then sent everyone off with the message "Have a good day!" We loved each encounter with him, and he brought smiles to our minivan. He was not "just a" ticket seller: he was an ambassador of joy.

People can make fantastic impressions in a simple way. When we shop at a warehouse store, a man in a wheelchair greets us. He says hello as he checks our ID. When I enter with my granddaughter, she likes to show him the membership card. She thinks this is an important job. The greeter understands this and makes a big fuss telling her that she was a big help and that she handed the card to him so well. She skips off smiling into the store, and I thank him for transmitting kindness and joy to a little girl. Being a greeter at a store might not seem impressive to many, but that job makes a big impression on me and our family.

I remember how impressive I felt when I got my first business card. Yes, I existed before I got five hundred of these cards with my name and contact information on them. Yet I somehow thought I needed them to prove I was somebody. When I brought them home, my children liked them because they pretended the cards were driver's licenses and other make-believe things. They did not need a small piece of cardstock for me to tell them who I was. Nor should I. But I did.

I'm reminded of my insecurity sometimes when I first meet someone. The inevitable questions start. Some are innocent questions, and many are sincere. But you know that, while the question-and-answer is happening, measurement and judgment are also at work.

Where did you go to school?

What do you do?

Where do you live?

What kind of car do you drive?

Where are you going on vacation?

What did you do this weekend?

Where did you get that coat?

The seemingly benign questions can carry so much weight, and make you feel as if you are being judged by all your answers. You wonder if people are just curious about your education or if they are judging you by the status of your school or the level of your education. And do people really want to know about your weekend, or do they judge how you spend your time? And when people ask what you do? Well, that question is a loaded one in so many ways. They might be making small talk or just trying to get to know you. Or they might be assessing you and your career choices.

I have met people who think they are not impressive because they have not traveled, but having a well-worn passport does not define a person. Awards are great, but a trophy shelf does not measure who you really are. And prizes are usually not given out to those who remember to bring a canned good to church for the parish food bank or say a prayer each night for those in need.

Saintly Inspiration

St. Anthony of Padua is known mainly as the saint to whom people pray when they lose things. This holy man, who was born in Portugal in 1195, is a great role model for those who fret about being impressive enough.

He became a Franciscan and dreamed about being a martyr but became sick in Africa and returned to Italy to live in the monastery. There he did menial work and did not have ambitions to become famous. In fact, this saint who was praised for his fine preaching was first ordered to give a sermon. He was not worried about being impressive when he wrote: "The spirit of humility is sweeter than honey, and those who nourish themselves with this honey produce sweet fruit."

It's good to know that you don't have to impress anyone to be loved. Your business card just has to read "Child of God." That is enough.

Putting Faith into Practice

- Here's another list challenge. Make a list of what impresses you the most about someone you know. Then make a list of what impresses you about yourself. How do those lists compare? Talk with God about each list.

- Make an effort to thank the service providers you encounter during your day. Be sure to thank the person who sold you your coffee or drove the school bus. Sometimes it seems easier to complain, but take the time to write a note of praise for someone who did a good job. Or post something positive on social media. However you communicate, be uplifting.

- If you know a teenager or a young adult, be extra kind. Give this person praise and express why you appreciate him or her.

Ignatian Examen

Give thanks.

Thank the Lord for whatever work you do each day. Do you volunteer? Raise children? Paint houses? Teach? Run a business? All of it is good. You are helping your family, yourself, and your community. Respect all labor and all titles. Be grateful to those who clean restrooms and sweep floors, and be grateful to those who search for cures for cancer. All impress in their own way.

Ask for the Spirit.

Ask the good Lord to help you be satisfied with your life right now. This does not mean that you cannot have goals or seek a new job or career. However, ask the Lord to help you recognize that your value does not have to come from what people think. And ask the Lord to keep you from constantly clicking on your screen and comparing.

Review and recognize challenges and failures.

Have you described yourself as "just a ____"? Or do you label people as "just a ____"? Do you value people by their job titles or resent people who have succeeded? It is hard to live in a world where status can convey power, and it is hard to figure out what really matters.

Ask for forgiveness and healing.

Ask God to help you understand that you were made to know, love, and serve God in this world and be happy with him in the next. Talk with God about your envy or your resentment over the good fortune of others. Talk with God about your anxiety and your fretting over "making it." Open your heart to humility and love.

Pray about tomorrow.

Try this prayer: *Dear Lord, do I impress you? It is good to know that I do not have to dazzle you for your love. Help me face tomorrow with a genuine sense of contentment that comes from not trying to be what I am not. Guide me to be the best I can be—but help me to sort out what that is. Motivate me to do what is best for me and not what looks good. And help me appreciate all the people who work together in this world to make it a place of love.*

8

Had Enough

*Do not become upset when difficulty comes your way. Laugh in its
face and know that you are in the hands of God.*
—St. Francis de Sales

When difficulty comes your way, you probably do not feel like laughing. Just think a moment about what you do when tough times come to your door. You don't have to write this down. But your immediate answer will reveal how you handle days when you've had enough.

When It's Your Turn

You let out a deep, long sigh and tap your fingers on the steering wheel. A funeral procession is rolling past and delaying your trip, and you are stuck at a light. You watch as a parade of cars goes by. Many of the cars are flying a little flag that says "Funeral." You keep hoping the next car will be without one. You know you should say a Hail Mary for the deceased and their family who mourns. A little part of you wonders who is in the hearse. You know you should not be impatient. But maybe you are in a hurry or just lacking patience, like myself, so you sigh. Finally the last car moves along and you continue on your trip to work, school, the grocery store, or home.

And then, one day, you are in the procession. You are not thinking about stopped traffic or delays. You look ahead at the hearse and just stare and wonder, *How am I going to live without my mom?* At least that's what I was thinking the first time great sorrow hit my life. It was a punch in the face, and I was reeling.

I had experienced some heartaches before that day. Boyfriends had broken my heart. Opportunities for jobs had passed me by. And a few beloved older relatives had died. But now I had lost my mother. This was the woman to whom I spoke on the phone several times a day. This was the woman I saw almost every day of my life. I would drop by with the kids to see her, and she would offer hugs, food, a listening ear, and a great interest in the ordinary. She loved to hear if one of the kids had said a new word or learned a new skill. And often she would come over with a treat for her grandchildren. Much to their delight, she gave them their first taste of Lucky Charms cereal. Of course, my dad came too, because he loved his grandchildren too, and my mother never learned to drive.

My mother was amazing. I loved her so much and told her as much so many times. However, I do not think that I appreciated her fully until she was gone. She gave birth to me late in life. It could not have been easy, but I never felt as if I were a surprise or burden. Of course, she guarded her age as though it were the nuclear code. I learned when I was much older that she was older than my father and did not like to share that fact with many people. She was active, youthful, always on the go, and never hampered by her lack of a license or the birthdate that would have been on it.

And on this sad, sunny June day, she was again being driven. This time it was by an employee of a funeral parlor. Trailing behind, in a car that held up traffic, I wondered what I would do without her.

As I grieved in the days that followed, I admit, I was a little frustrated with God. I thought God was my friend and felt that he had let me down. He had become my pal when my mother introduced me to him at a very young age. She loved God with her whole heart and spent a lot of time with him. I have very early memories of going with my mom to the Miraculous Medal novenas on Monday afternoons at our parish church. She recited the prayers, and I slid around on the pew and looked about. Church became a familiar and comfortable place for me because of her. It was just one of many, many trips to church or parish functions I attended with her and my dad. She took pride when her baked goods were eaten up at a guild meeting. She attended daily Mass and prayed—a lot. She had a giant Ziploc bag filled with prayer cards, novenas, and memorial cards from wakes. Throughout her life she offered prayers for me and all her loved ones. Not only did she pray for me, but she also encouraged me to pray. She set an example every time she broke out her rosary beads on every long car ride, much to my youthful dismay. She had lived through the Great Depression, World War II, and so many changing times, but she was steadfast in her belief that, to quote Julian of Norwich, "All shall be well, and all shall be well, and all manner of things shall be well."

Perhaps the only thing she did to make me really angry and doubt her beloved God was to leave me. She left me and my dad and my brother and sister on a quiet Friday evening. She was not young—seventy-nine—but she should have had some more years, and I wanted her to see my children grow up. I wanted to share more Sunday dinners, more phone calls, more laughs, and more moments of prayer.

I was thirty-seven when she died—neither young nor old. I knew there were many people who had lost their moms at a much earlier age. But at that moment, all I knew was that I wanted my mommy. That summer was the only time I lost weight without trying. I kept things going. I shuttled my children to games and school and read to them at night. I did the laundry. My father came to dinner several times a week. He was hurting more than I was, but he was more consoled by his faith. I was not. Sometimes I was mad at God and resentful that my peers still had their parents.

God's Messengers

Then God sent a messenger. The message did not come from an angel but from my angelic four-year-old daughter, Elizabeth. After weeks of watching me be sad, she looked at me one morning and said, "Are we going to do something today or are we going to sit around and cry?" Wow! Her words struck me hard and made me realize that I needed to mourn differently and take a hard look at myself.

Grief tests you, but, if you let it, then it transforms you. I can think back now on those blurry, tear-filled days and not cry. Back then I couldn't make it through the grocery store without seeing something that reminded me of my mom and starting to blubber. But as I worked my way through it, I am grateful for the fact that I did not give up on God.

In fact, during that difficult time, I turned to God often, even when I was upset with him. I clung and prayed to him when I didn't quite know why. Two years later, though, another unpleasant surprise came my way. My dad was given a diagnosis of terminal cancer. I thought: *Seriously, God, what is your plan here? Do you want to rip my heart out altogether?* Again, I was angry. My father was such a good, kind man. Since my mother's death, we had spent even more time together. We loved him so much. How were we all going to cope with this loss? *Why?* I asked the air, because it felt that I was praying to a faraway God.

Again, a messenger came, only this time it was Dad himself. As we accompanied him through his last months, we tried to do extra-nice things for him. One weekend we went with him to my brother's lake home. When it was bedtime, I knocked on his door to check on him and bid him goodnight. There was no answer, and I felt panicked. *Dear God,* I thought, *has he collapsed on the floor or died in his sleep?* I worried about all the grandchildren gathered there. Taking a deep breath, I slowly opened the door. Fearful, I expected to see the worst.

Instead, I saw something so beautiful and memorable. There was my father, on his knees, next to the bed, saying his night prayers. Weakened by cancer, aware of his impending death, he still made the effort to kneel and talk with his Creator that night. I was moved to tears and entered the room. I helped him to his feet and hugged him. My dad showed me that, during the darkest times in life, sometimes the only thing you can do is pray. Or maybe it is the only thing you *should* do. Either way, I have clung to that memory of my dad and tried to pray daily, and I wish I did it more often on my knees.

And then life goes on and there are ups and downs. There are job losses. There are car troubles. There are more losses. And they hurt and trouble you, but they do not sting as much as the loss of your parents. And then comes another suffocating time when you feel that you have had enough, way more than enough. You feel like Job from the Old Testament, who cried out: "When I lie down I say, 'When shall I arise?' Then the night drags on; I am filled with restlessness until the dawn." Or you want to shout his woeful comment: "Remember that my life is like the wind; my eye will not see happiness again."

You just sit and wonder why some things happen. You wonder why. *Why, Lord?*

Perhaps this has happened to you. We get really bad news, and we do not understand why things are happening. We want to bargain with God. We say we will never swear or eat ice cream again if the test results come back differently. We cry. We hurt. And we feel lost and abandoned. We are in a fog and cannot see a path, never mind an end to our misery. We are told to trust and pray, but we do not have the energy for it.

My husband and I felt this way and asked God why as we watched our daughter and her husband endure a beautiful and terrible suffering. We were in awe as we saw them be brave and noble and good amid doctors' visits and ultrasounds. And we were with them as they endured an incredible, unbelievably difficult heartache on a sad September day when their beloved and beautiful daughter Marian Elizabeth, our first grandchild, died the day she was born.

This experience tested my faith. My husband and I sobbed that day and held each other tight and asked where God was when we had prayed for healing of our tiniest loved one. Our miracle did not happen, and the loss was and still is a mystery to our family. But God's messenger was Marian's mother, our daughter Elizabeth, who conducted herself with such dignity and courage and grace. As long as I live, I will never forget how strong and good and loving she was. God was there through the tears and the sorrow and in the beautiful example of motherhood embodied in our daughter.

A week later, we said, "You've really got to be kidding, God," when I got a phone call that our son was heading into emergency surgery. He had to have most of his stomach removed in a lengthy surgery and nearly died.* It was 4 a.m. as I headed to Boston; I can still recall the feeling of driving too fast on the Massachusetts Turnpike. I was rushing and praying, "Please, God, let him be okay." But a part of me thought, *He might not be okay. I know bad things happen, so why would I be exempt today from heartache? I have prayed before for favors and not gotten the answer I wanted. I have faced great sorrow. Will it be another difficult day?* Fortunately, Matthew was okay, but I knew from other times that God does not always answer our prayers in the way we want or expect. And that is when we must think about what we believe and, more importantly, how well we trust.

---

* You can read about this experience in the book *Operating on Faith* by Matthew Weber, Loyola Press.

Blessed Are They Who Mourn

The Beatitudes say: Blessed are they who mourn, for they shall be comforted. Those words should make you feel better, but most of the time you think, *I do not want to be one of those who are blessed. I want my loved one back!* Or your health back or your job back. And then another day passes, and you realize that mourning takes time. It takes a lot of time. But you can tell yourself that the next day will not be as tough, and you can believe that your spirit is resilient. So, the company that employed you for thirty years has just let you go. Or you just found out that a loved one needs heart surgery. Or you feel overwhelmed and anxious and ready to scream. You can say, *Enough, God, enough.*

Tragic events happen somewhere in the world every day. Of the many people suffering, there is no way of measuring whose pain is worse. Each person handles hardship in his or her own way. But most agree that the loss of a child is exceptionally hard and unnatural. Families who endure that kind of pain experience great testing of their faith. Their patience is tested too. It is especially hard when well-meaning people say things like "I know how you feel" or "God must have wanted him." Ultimately, no one understands why suffering or misery happens.

Sorrow Can Transform

Job said to God, when he finally got it: "By hearsay I had heard of you, but now my eye has seen you. Therefore I disown what I have said, and repent in dust and ashes." Job had an encounter with God that transformed him and made him see his suffering in a completely different light. It can happen. So many people see their hardship or heartache transformed into something beautiful. They take the unbearable and create an incredible example of faith or hope or love, or all three. Bud Welch was one of those people. In 1995, his twenty-three-year-old daughter was killed in the bombing of the Alfred P. Murrah Federal Building in Oklahoma City. She was one of 168 people who died senselessly at the hands of Timothy McVeigh and Terry Nichols. Nichols was sentenced to life in prison and McVeigh was executed in 2001.

Bud has said that he was bitter and angry after his daughter's death. He sought vengeance and began to drink heavily. However, he received an epiphany. I would call it God's grace. He came to realize that it was hate that caused the terror attack—and he had to stop hating. He began to speak out against the death penalty. He even met McVeigh's father. And Bud said that about a year before McVeigh was executed, he was able to forgive his daughter's killer.

I do not know if I would be able to do what Bud Welch did. I would like to think I could, but I also know I have held grudges and nursed hurts over much smaller offenses. I know I have viewed prayer like a bank account and expected a return on my Hail Marys. And I know that I really do not understand why suffering exists and why such sad things happen to so many people.

But, through all my own heartaches I have come to rely on God as my source of comfort, consolation, and hope. And I have seen the face of God in people who have offered me a kind word, a casserole, or the squeeze of a hand. I have watched groups of people knit prayer shawls for happy times but also for sad times. These warm, wooly hugs are sent to those who might be enduring chemotherapy or mourning the death of a loved one. God is in all things and all people.

Every time I am ready to throw in the towel or say I have had enough, God says, "Hang on." The Catholic Catechism says this quite well: "The desire for God is written in the human heart, because man is created by God and for God; and God never ceases to draw man to himself. Only in God will he find the truth and happiness he never stops searching for" (No. 27).

Saintly Inspiration

We can look to St. Elizabeth Ann Seton as someone who could have given up on God. She is known as the patron saint of grief. Her husband died after going through a long illness. Elizabeth was left with five children. She then lost two of her children and most of her wealth and her standing in society. When she became Catholic, she was ostracized by many of her friends. She stayed with God. Father Joseph Esper notes in his essay about grief that after St. Elizabeth's husband died, she was able to pray, "I know that these contradictory events are permitted by your wisdom, which solely is light. We are in darkness and must be thankful that our knowledge is not wanted to perfect your work."

She did not know why bad things happened, but she kept going and ended up establishing the first Catholic school in the United States and founding the Sisters of Charity. When she had had enough, she turned to God. It is a simple yet difficult solution. We just have to turn to God when we have had enough.

Putting Faith into Practice

- Pull out a photo album or your phone. Look at the faces in it and be glad for the people who have been with you in joy or sorrow.
- Think about someone you need to forgive and try and do it. Maybe going to confession will help.
- If someone has helped you through a rough patch, thank that person. Even if you did so a while ago, thank that person again. Your appreciation will be welcome. It also might encourage you to be the person of support for someone else.
- Have a Mass said for a loved one. Or visit the cemetery. These can be moments of pain, but they also can be moments of prayer and love.

Ignatian Examen

Give thanks.

Thank the Lord for those who have helped you through the difficult times in your life. Whether a stranger who paid for your coffee or a friend who sat with you for hours, appreciate that person. He or she is the face of God and a great source of comfort and inspiration.

Ask for the Spirit.

Ask the good Lord to help you through the tough moments, when getting out of bed seems to be too much. Recite the Serenity Prayer so that you have "the serenity to accept the things you cannot change, the courage to change the things you can, and the wisdom to know the difference."

Review and recognize challenges and failures.

When have you held grudges and been mad at others or God? What step can you take to let go of the should-haves and could-haves? How can you see God's grace and presence in your dark times?

Ask for forgiveness and healing.

Ask God to help you forgive those who have caused you pain. Ask forgiveness for all the times you have struck out in anger from your own hurt. Seek healing through counseling, prayer, exercise, quiet, music, or whatever it takes to get you through the periods in your life when you have had enough.

Pray about tomorrow.

Try this prayer: *Dear Lord, sometimes I just can't take it. Help me get through those difficult days and see your goodness, even when the days are dark. Help me see you in the people and world around me. Guide me to make the most of life, even when it is not going well. And help me celebrate all the people I miss and all they have taught me.*

9

Quiet Enough

Never be in a hurry; do everything quietly and in a calm spirit.
Do not lose your inner peace for anything whatsoever, even if your
whole world seems upset.
—St. Francis de Sales

It's time to turn down the music and shut off your phone. I invite you to take a few deep breaths and get ready to think about what is quiet enough in your life. You can jot down where you like to go to think. You can list your favorite churches—usually quiet places. And then you can begin to see that finding quiet might be quite what you need.

The Quiet Game

Throughout my lifetime I have visited many places; however, none of them has been particularly exotic. But it would be fair to say that a few of them could fall into the category of unusual for most people, because I have been inside more than my fair share of convents. Having a sister who was a nun certainly gave me an inside track. She was a Sister of St. Joseph for almost fifty years before her death. I also have written "day-in-the-life" stories about some cloistered communities. We even lived across the street from our parish convent. The main reason my convent knowledge is so extensive is that it started early in life. My mother knew a lot of nuns, and we went to see them. We visited cloistered nuns and what I called "the regular kind" of nuns throughout my childhood. In particular, we often spent time with Sister Mary Modesta, one of my mother's former teachers. We often would travel to wherever she was stationed and spend a Sunday afternoon there. This kind of weekend activity was not my first choice, but we really had no choice. My brother and I were little and had to come along. We were dressed up and put in the back of the car, where we got ourselves ready for the convent parlor routine.

Upon our arrival, we were greeted by Sister. She inquired about our life and then reached under the white bib of her habit and pulled out a watch. It was like a train conductor's watch, and she pointed to the hands of the clock. "The quiet game will now begin," she said, with a smile. The first rule of the quiet game was pretty obvious: You had to keep quiet. You were allowed to check with Sister every so often about how much longer you had to remain silent. We were asked to not utter a word for an hour. Sister Modesta gave us periodic updates about how much time we had left. She would tell us when we had a half hour to go or let us know that only a few minutes remained.

We came prepared for the quiet game. We brought books, crayons, paper, and other things to keep us busy. But sometimes it was quite hard to be quiet. It seems that you always want to talk when you can't. This happens for the same reason you always crave a cheeseburger on a Friday in Lent. And enforced silence is hard when you are a chatterbox like me. I felt that I was bursting by the end of the hour. The "game" was perfect for the grown-ups. Their visit was not interrupted by us yapping away. Surprisingly, I also do not recall listening to them. I cannot remember their conversations. But I can easily think back to those times of having to be quiet.

I did manage to be silent for the hour. This was not because I was so good; nor was I quiet because I appreciated the silence. No, it was the other rule of the quiet game that kept me from talking. Rule 2: If you kept quiet for the whole hour, then you got cookies and soda.

And you also got to walk with Sister Modesta to the kitchen to help carry the items. This meant that you got to see the inner workings of the convent. You passed by the activity room, the sun porch, and even the dining room to get to the kitchen. During this trek to the inner sanctum, you might even get a glimpse of a nun wearing an apron. Since the insides of a convent were a huge mystery to all children of my era, the idea of peeking behind the curtain to see real convent life was definitely worth keeping my mouth shut for sixty minutes.

After the cookies had been eaten and the ginger ale sipped from cute little glasses, we would get ready to leave. Sometimes Sister gave us a pencil or some other parting gift. But we already were leaving with a gift, even though we didn't realize it at the time: We had been silent, and that allowed our parents to have some peace. We had the satisfaction of being in control of ourselves, our voices, and our impulses for 3,600 seconds. And we were beginning to learn how to appreciate quiet—enforced or not.

The Importance of Quiet

It has been a slow journey for me to fully appreciate quiet since my time in the convent parlor. I now see how important it is to have silence in my life. Being quiet and embracing the need for quiet have always been challenging for me. It remains a struggle, despite my growing appreciation for time without sound or distraction. I love to talk with people. I will talk with strangers just about anywhere. I chat up people in line in the grocery store. I talk to people on the train. My daughter Kerry tells me that few people strike up conversations with strangers on Amtrak—but I do. No quiet car for me! And I love long phone calls with friends. Add a cup of coffee, and I'm in a little corner of heaven. A cookie or scone would complete that celestial picture. But of course these conversations are two-way streets; I also love to listen to people's stories. I find the ordinary life to be extraordinary and will happily listen to someone tell me about her family or work or vacation or how he found a great bargain at a store with extra coupons and savvy shopping.

I keep working on appreciating quiet, and time alone is something I have learned to value more. Wanting solitude does not mean that I have become shy. I do not mind speaking in public and will chat away at any table at which I am seated at a wedding. But I do find myself shutting off the TV more often, just to sit and think and sometimes pray. I am a long way from the point at which I could do this all day. I do like the idea of making chocolates like the Trappistine Nuns in Wrentham, Massachusetts, but I cannot imagine living their lifestyle of prayer and silence. My father joked that if I ever decided to join, it would take only sixty minutes before I had to leave or get tossed out. When I was younger, those entering the strict religious community lived an almost completely silent life. Today it is not one of absolute silence, but they take a vow of conversion that includes celibacy, fasting, manual labor, separation from the world, and silence. They practice what they call a "radical silence."

Today, a life of silence *is* radical. It is a life that most people could not imagine. It seems that everyone is surrounded by dinging, ringing headphones, earbuds, and boxes like Alexa and Google that talk back to you. Most people have a hard time being separated from their cell phones, and many sleep with them beside their bed. The world is noisier and busier, and people are bombarded by sounds and images. So many people have problems with stress, sleep, high blood pressure, anxiety, and overall fatigue. Stores, restaurants, airports, and many public places are filled with music and TV screens. No wonder so many of us are beginning to crave more quiet.

Sometimes we experience the illusion of quiet. After my grandson Cillian was born, I would frequently ride a train from New York City to Hoboken, New Jersey, to visit my daughter and her family. You could hear a pin drop on the train. No one was talking. But it was not the stillness of church or the sleepy quiet of travel. Everyone was looking at his or her phone or some other device. Most people had earbuds in their ears. A few rare souls were reading books. But no one looked at anyone. It was so strange. This was not quiet. This was isolation and a lack of being present to anyone. I found it so strange and a little sad.

So, what is enough quiet, and how do we find the quiet we need?

Finding Quiet

We do not have to join a convent or a monastery, but we could commit to a little peace and quiet every day. For me, sometimes it is clicking off the radio in the car and just driving. No music, just me. Suddenly I notice the flowers in bloom and pay more attention as I move along the streets. I think more. My thoughts might wander, but sometimes those thoughts yield an inspiration. Other times I create a mental to-do list or plan a meal. Whatever happens, my thoughts have had a chance to rattle around and my mind has had a chance to stretch itself.

Finding quiet might mean popping into church for a quick prayer. Visiting a church is one of my favorite things to do. I love the light and the silence. My dad used to take my kids to his parish church to say hello to God. It might not have been the quietest visit when they went, but stopping by a church has always been a nice thing to do in our family. I have found church to be a peaceful and calming place of beauty, where one can sit for a moment and pause.

Finding quiet can take many other forms. For some it means a retreat. The Jesuits have many retreat houses, and several specialize in silent retreats. They note on one retreat house website that "silence is essential to achieving the stillness where a person meets God." You won't see me signing up for a silent retreat. I cannot fathom living in silence for a week, never mind twenty-one days. But I am learning the value of being quiet enough—for me, for now.

The older I get, the more I appreciate quiet. It seems that with the onslaught of devices like cell phones, laptop computers, tablets, and TV screens—even in cars—noise is everywhere. Work never ends because I can get a text or receive an e-mail on my phone. Every time I sit down at the computer, someone tries to sell me something with a targeted ad or an e-mail.

Quiet is a true need. Just as we might crave a salad after eating too many rich foods during the holidays, we want quiet after being bombarded with dinging phones and news alerts. Even Jesus showed the need for quiet when "he would withdraw to deserted places and pray" (Luke 5:16.) The Lord himself had to find a place of solitude. We all do. Maybe for you it is going to the ocean or climbing a hill. Perhaps sitting in a library or museum is your cup of tea. Or maybe it is just sitting and having a cup of tea that quiets you down. Quiet comes, but we must invite it.

As I grow in my appreciation of quiet, I also admire people who are more self-contained and comfortable with quiet. I love how my husband takes time to think for a while before he speaks. He does not blurt out his thoughts the way I sometimes do. And I have learned to sit with him in what could be called companionable silence. It is nice to simply be in the car and drive along without the need to talk. And then, after a bit, it is nice to share what we have been thinking.

We All Need Quiet

The funny thing about silence and quiet is that sometimes you do not know how much you need it until you experience how fruitful it can be. Each of us must figure out how much quiet is enough for us. Quiet is healing. Quiet is good. And it can yield powerful results.

Gage Park High School in Chicago instituted quiet time for twenty minutes each morning and afternoon. Some argued that students could use the time for more classroom work and that the practice should not take away valuable learning time. But the program yielded big benefits. In the life of teens in a big city, there is so much noise, and it can be deafening and overwhelming. This quiet time was a respite for them. The school found that the quiet time was healing and helpful, that it reduced stress among the students and the faculty. Students were shown how to meditate, and some did. Others slept or just sat still. Yet, almost all seemed to appreciate the break in the day and the opportunity to be still. Suspensions were down at the school, and students and faculty alike reported that they could cope better and were less angry. The quiet helped.

Instinctively, people appreciate quiet and understand it. I recall my visit to the Grand Canyon in Arizona. It is a magnificent place, often dubbed "God's natural cathedral." Crowds of tourists milled about, staring out at the vast and magnificent view. But it was not a raucous time. People spoke in hushed tones as if they recognized the beauty and majesty of this natural wonder. Beauty often evokes quiet. It's as if the brain needs the quiet to process what it takes in through the physical senses.

When you hold a sleeping baby, you tend to be quiet even though most newborns are not disturbed by noise. Rather, the quiet and the calm come from holding in your arms a miracle of creation. It is astonishing to look at the tiny human and realize that he or she emerged from the mother's womb and is now here to grow in wisdom and grace and love. There are no words for this amazing experience other than a coo and an *I love you.*

Why So Much Noise?

I remember my college years, when students' stereos would be turned up, blasting out of dorm windows. You got used to the noise. However, one Dominican priest took note and mentioned it in a homily about quiet. Citing the mathematician and philosopher René Descartes, he noted that these students were Cartesians. Only the ones blaring their stereos were not saying, "I think; therefore I am"; rather, according to the priest, "They think they *are* because they *hear*." In other words, the constant sound affirmed that they were there. It's a great point. People make noise for lots of reasons—sometimes good ones. But often, people shout or yell or cheer because they want to be heard or acknowledged. "Pay attention to me. Listen to me," is the message of a lot of people today. And this is understandable. But you have to be sure that you do not follow the rule that "he or she who is loudest wins." And you have to provide a place for people to whisper what is in the quiet of their hearts.

So, whisper what is in your heart right now. And then take another deep breath and listen to the world around you.

Right now, I can hear birds chirping. I know that a mother bird has placed five eggs in a nest near our front door. I marvel at this. But I am not always quiet about this or immune to the urge to tweet, call, or ping others to tell them about our avian visitors. We take photos of this wonderful spring happening and text it to our family. Technology can be useful. It is a kind of noise, but it can be good. Noise is not always bad. We must try to find the balance and live a deliberate life in which we make room and time for quiet.

Saintly Inspiration

The great writer and monk Thomas Merton understood the importance of quiet. Merton was a convert to Catholicism and a poet and a truly fascinating man. He wrote many books after entering the Abbey of Gethsemani in Kentucky in 1941. Perhaps his most famous was *The Seven Storey Mountain*, an autobiography describing how he came to live as a Trappist monk. His works focused on many themes, but most involved the spiritual life. And his life of work, austerity, and silence gave him the opportunity to do much reflecting and writing. It was his superior who encouraged his writing and publication.

In 1955, Merton wrote *No Man Is an Island*, and had this to say about quiet: "If we strive to be happy by filling all the silence of life with sound, productive by turning all life's leisure into work, and real by turning all our being into doing, we will only succeed in producing a hell on earth."

Clearly Merton is encouraging us to be still, to be present, and to be ourselves. Quiet is part of that process, and once you figure out how to be quiet enough, you will be on the way to feeling that you are enough.

Putting Faith into Practice

- If you can, schedule a retreat. It probably won't be easy to carve time out of your schedule, but don't give up. If you can't get away, try to schedule a few minutes of your day to be still. Take the time to just sit in quiet for a few minutes with no expectations. Maybe get some support from a friend. Just as friends who want to exercise more or eat better help each other out, enlist the support from another to embrace how you can be quiet enough.

- Use your devices to set an alarm once a day that reminds you to stop, breathe, and pray.

- Plan a trip to a different church or a shrine to capture a moment of quiet and a new spiritual experience.

- Check out a library book by Thomas Merton and see if he speaks to you.

Ignatian Examen

Give thanks.

Thank the Lord for all that you see and hear. And then thank the Lord for moments of quiet, brief though many may be. Thank the Lord for what might be revealed in the quiet.

Ask for the Spirit.

Ask the Lord to help you stop making excuses and start carving out time, even just a few minutes, to be still, present, and quiet. Ask the Lord to help you truly hear and discern.

Review and recognize challenges and failures.

Have you surrounded yourself with devices and dings and noise? Are you tethered to constant updates and messages? Do you worry that if you are not "connected," you do not count? Have you given up on finding quiet and just figured it is not possible or suitable to your lifestyle? Are you afraid of quiet and what you might hear once the noise is gone?

Ask for forgiveness and healing.

Ask the Lord to help you truly listen to him. Give him a chance to speak to you. Open your heart and listen to what is going on in your life and what you need. Be honest about how you sometimes resist being quiet and why. Ask to find healing in the quiet.

Pray about tomorrow.

Try this prayer: *Dear Lord, please help me find quiet in my life. Help me listen better to others and to you. Help me rid my life—even for a short time—of all the sounds and devices that keep me from attending to what is important. Help me find the quiet that fits my life and situation.*

10
Holy Enough

*All of us can attain to Christian virtue and holiness, no matter in
what condition of life we live and no matter what our life's
work might be.*
—St. Francis de Sales

You can write this one down or just think about it: What or who
is a holy person? Or, what makes a person holy? Perhaps your first
response is, *Not me—I'm not holy.* Upon further reflection, you might
identify the qualities you admire in holy people. And if you are willing
to think just a bit harder, you might find what path to holiness you
will choose.

An Early and Epic Fail

Friday nights were special when I was a kid. Homework could wait
until the next day. Our newspaper route was done, and we had a few
coins in our pockets. We also got to watch TV in the living room and
eat some snacks in there. Watching television was delightful because
we were not allowed to do so on school nights. But on Fridays, we
warmed up the set, adjusted the antenna, and got ready to be enter-
tained. We were allowed to eat in the living room only on special
occasions, so, clearly, Fridays were special. It was so much fun to settle
into the sofa and watch our shows. We would open a bottle of soda

and eat potato chips and feel like we were having a wonderful night of treats, both visually and gastronomically.

For a while, the *Flintstones* cartoon was our special Friday-night show. The prime-time prehistoric animation would come roaring into our home, and we would all laugh at the adventures of the caveman family and the antics of dear Fred. I think back fondly on my Friday nights. But the theme song of the *Flintstones* still causes me a brief pang of guilt when I hear it because it was that show that first made me think I was not holy enough.

As an earnest fifth grader, I wanted to be a good and sincere Catholic. I read books about the saints, and my teachers tried to inspire us to make sacrifices and to become better people. So, one Lent I made up my mind to show my spiritual mettle and go big. I decided to give up everything. My list included no candy, no soda, no chips, and *no* television. This was going to be the mother of all Lents, and I was going to greet Easter like a true holy kid in the making.

Ash Wednesday was not a problem. After all, the big cross of burnt palms on my forehead was a very visible reminder to be good. The next day, I craved a little candy, but we usually did not have many treats around the house during Lent, so I was able to resist temptation. And then came Friday. This was my first real test of holiness. The TV came on, and the family settled into the living room to watch our shows and munch on snacks. I nobly left the room to head upstairs and read. At the doorway, I heard the fizz of the soda and the crackle as it connected to the ice cubes. I smelled the chips and imagined their salty crunch. And as I was three steps up, the theme song began: "Flintstones, meet the Flintstones . . ." I paused on the steps, frozen on the landing. I reasoned that I could listen to the show. After all, I had only given up *watching* television, not listening to it. The rationalizing continued. I crept down a few steps to hear the TV better. However, I heard something that made everyone laugh, but I did not understand what was so funny. It would be okay, I thought, to just take a peek.

The next thing I knew, I was kneeling on the floor in the living room and watching the show and laughing with the family. I had blown my Lenten resolution, and we had not even celebrated the First Sunday in Lent. Sighing, I went to the kitchen during a commercial and grabbed my soda and bowl of chips. Done! I had caved in on the third day of Lent. I was done with Lent. After that experience, I determined that I was not a teensy bit holy, and I knew that I would never be a saint. St. Margaret of Springfield was not going to ever happen—ever.

Of course, I can say now that I had unrealistic expectations and that I had to learn that being holy and good involves a lot more than giving up potato chips and TV. Since my Lent as a ten-year-old, I have experienced many more Lents. During each one, I try to recapture my zeal for being holy. However, each Lent—some more than others—I worry that I am not living my faith to the fullest and that I'm still not quite holy enough. Could I really be holy if I skipped daily Mass to sleep later? Could I be holy if I kept making excuses for why I had not been to confession in a while? Could I be holy if I rationalized that a chocolate doughnut is not a sweet—it's a breakfast food? Could I be holy if I barely prayed the rosary or novenas? Wouldn't a holy person volunteer more at soup kitchens and give more to charity? And certainly, truly holy people would not think that Lent might be a good way to drop ten pounds. I have felt and thought all those things, and I know that I'm trying and that there is no one formula for living a holy life. But I still have quite often felt I was not holy enough.

Notions of Perfection

It can be so hard to shake that feeling of inadequacy when it comes to your spiritual life. You know that you do not have to be perfect. Yet you also know that there are people who pray a lot more, do a lot more, and know a lot more than you do. You can, like me, take comfort in the words of Pope Francis, who said aboard the papal plane in July 2013 as he spoke to the press: "St. Peter committed one of the greatest sins, denying Christ, and yet they made him pope. Think about that." You know God is forgiving and loves you. You know you can always try again. But the underlying feelings of spiritual inadequacy trip you up.

I have had conversations with people who have lectured me about what I need to do to be "a good Catholic." Many well-intentioned Catholics have stressed that Eucharistic adoration is the most meaningful activity anyone can do and that every person should do it. I have come to appreciate the quiet and beauty of that devotion, but I also know that I sometimes get squirmy sitting there. I know I should be in awe of the Eucharist, but my mind wanders and then I think that all the other people are having beatific visions while I consider what I am going to do once this prayer time is over.

And I have had conversations with truly good people who have emphasized the importance of doing good works. They stress that making meals and helping the poor in some way is the most meaningful activity any person can do. And I appreciate the power of witness and the ways we can recognize Jesus while serving others. I know I should go out more and do more, but I don't. I see so many dedicated people who volunteer many hours each week, but I am more of a homebody who will bake for others and make donations but not make a habit of venturing out to shelters or jails or other places the way so many others do.

In *Gaudete Et Exsultate: On the Call to Holiness in Today's World*, an apostolic exhortation by Pope Francis, he reminds us that there are many paths to holiness:

> We should not grow discouraged before examples of holiness that appear unattainable. There are some testimonies that may prove helpful and inspiring, but that we are not meant to copy, for that could even lead us astray from the one specific path that the Lord has in mind for us. The important thing is that each believer discern his or her own path, that they bring out the very best of themselves, the most personal gifts that God has placed in their hearts (cf. *1 Cor* 12:7), rather than hopelessly trying to imitate something not meant for them. We are all called to be witnesses, but there are many actual ways of bearing witness.

Those words are such a comfort. You do not have to be a bishop or a priest or start a religious community or even have a statue of Mary in your yard to be holy. I admit a fondness for religious items, and the Blessed Mother graces our yard and our kitchen counter. Her presence is a great witness for us, but it might not be for everyone. God desires that you walk *your* path to holiness. Certainly, you can look to the saints for examples. I remember doing that as a child, but I also remember wanting to be holy but not so holy that the Blessed Mother would appear to me! I thought that the kids who had those visions had a really hard time, and I did not want that. I wanted to be good—just regular good.

I have spent a lot of my life trying to figure out what being good means. I have done various kinds of volunteer work and made meals for the poor and tutored children in need. And I have tried to pray the rosary daily and attend Mass frequently. But I have come to realize that my vocations are as a mother, wife, and writer. Those are the vocations that will lead me to become *regular good*.

A key lesson for me has been that, no matter what you do, God has to be at the heart of your path to holiness and that any good you do must be connected to prayer. Mother Teresa said:

> Faith in action is service. We try to be holy because we believe. In most modern rooms you see an electrical light that can be turned on with a switch. But, if there is no connection with the main powerhouse, then there can be no light. Faith and prayer are the connection with God, and when that is there, there is service.
>
> —*No Greater Love* by Mother Teresa, 1977

When my daughter Elizabeth went on a service trip during high school, she and her fellow students did many good deeds during their trip. They sorted donations at a place that provided clothing for those in need. And they went out to the streets of Philadelphia to hand out hot dogs on a chilly Friday night. However, their campus minister understood the connection between God and helping others. He had the group of teens sit before the Eucharist in prayer before handing out the food. He wanted them to understand that they would be the hands of Christ that night and that they were not just doing good: they were doing a corporal work of mercy. That lesson was a strong one, for my daughter and for me. I realized that as I struggled to be holy enough, I had to ask God for help and understanding, that God had to be at the core of whatever task I did.

Avoid Complacency

As much as I do not feel holy enough, I know that sometimes I can feel superior to others or even smug. I will watch reality TV while pedaling on my exercise bike and watch a parade of people doing things I would never do. I will sit there, sweating away, and think, *Well, at least I'm not on TV with people who are screaming about the paternity of a baby or spending $10,000 on a wedding dress.* And then I stop, most of the time, and remind myself that we all journey toward

God in our own way and in our own time. Who am I to judge who is holy and how or when they take that path? Think about how many times people make comments about those who come to church only on Christmas and Easter. Ask yourself if you extend a warm welcome to those who have been away from the church for a while. St. Augustine, one of the great doctors of the church, came to the Lord after a life of debauchery and sin. No one said, "Sorry, Augie, you really have been a bad boy and don't belong here." It's important to recognize that everyone will be on his or her own path to holiness.

And, I must admit, I wonder where my path will lead. Would I have the courage of a martyr? In 2013, a group of terrorists killed more than 60 shoppers at a mall in Kenya. The shooters specifically targeted Christians. It was reported that if the people said they were not Christians, they were spared. I wonder what I would have done. Would I have stood by my faith or would I have been like St. Peter and denied Christ?

I do not know, but one thing I am certain of is that my faith has been blessed by great guides. I have been surrounded by some truly holy people. The ones I admire most are those who do not think they are holy. They simply go about doing good. My husband is one of those people. He happily fixes things for others and offers how-to advice to anyone who asks. He uses his incredible skills and knowledge to assist anyone in need. He has done this his whole life. Second Corinthians describes him: "for God loves a cheerful giver" (9:7).

I also like to say that I am the cheese in a saintly sandwich. My parents are the top slice of bread. They were quiet and loving saints who provided me with a love of God and an example of how to be kind. They gave rides to others. They made meals for those who were grieving. They prayed. They volunteered. My dad was an usher, a lector, a Eucharistic minister, and even the parish bingo caller. And my dad would play the piano at the end of many parish dances to keep the party going and inspire a sing-along. My mom baked for anybody and everybody. She invited a myriad of people to our holiday celebrations so those people would not be alone. And dear Hank and Connie gave generously even though they did not have much. Every payday they set aside the money to go in the church envelope. They truly used the talents they had to lead holy lives.

The bottom slice of bread in my saint sandwich? My children. My daughter Kerry spent a year helping children with special needs while volunteering in the Navajo Nation with the Sisters of Mercy. She studied, prayed, and became a Mercy Associate. My son has used his media skills to spread the word of God (even winning an Emmy) and performs random acts of kindness almost daily. And my daughter Elizabeth's thirst for knowledge about her faith and her way of explaining it to others is remarkable. Her stunning example of love for her Marian was amazing.

My parents, my husband, my children—all of them in their own way show me how to be holy, and they demonstrate that everyone can be holy enough as they embrace the best way to live. You just have to look around your world and figure out your way.

Saintly Inspiration

St. Francis de Sales clearly is one of my favorite saints. His words in his books are so clear and sincere. His book *Introduction to the Devout Life* is filled with great quotes. He lived from 1567 to 1622, but his advice has just as much relevance today. He lived during a time when people thought that only clergy or those in religious life could attain real holiness. He said that everyone could be holy. This was a radical thought for his time, but it resonated with many people then and continues to do so now. He offered spiritual direction to all. He said that all were called to holiness.

And he called all to embrace the faith. He spent much of his life living near Calvinists. He decided to knock on the doors of those people and try to lead them back to the Catholic faith. When people would not open their doors, he would write out pamphlets. And he would be kind to their children to set a good example. He did this for three years. His persistence and personal touch worked. It is said he led forty thousand people back to the Catholic faith. His path is probably not one that most of us would take, but it is a path that was genuine and caring.

We can listen to the words of St. Francis de Sales, who said, most famously, "Be who you are and be that perfectly well."

If you take that advice, then you will be able to figure out the way to be holy enough.

Putting Faith into Practice

- Ask yourself if you're happy with the state of your spiritual life and/or where your spiritual life is headed.

- Then determine what you can do to become holier. Do you want to pray more? Do you want to volunteer more? Try reading parts of Pope Francis's exhortation on holiness. Just do a little at a time. Then take a chance. Volunteer somewhere if you are drawn to that charism.

- Pick up a book on the spiritual life or sit in front of the Eucharist once a week. Say, "I am holy because I am a child of God." And look around and tell others that you admire their holiness. It will nurture you and your community.

Ignatian Examen

Give thanks.

Thank the Lord for all the holy people who have provided good examples. It is so nice to look around and see how each person finds his or her own way to God.

Ask for the Spirit.

Ask the Lord to guide you on your path. Evaluate your own gifts and talents and figure out how you can serve others in *your* best possible way.

Review and recognize challenges and failures.

Recognize your foibles and failures. Do you give up easily? Are you too hard on yourself? Do you feel that you are not holy enough? Do you feel better than others? Ask for God's guidance as you strive for holiness.

Ask for forgiveness and healing.

Ask God to help you forgive yourself for all the times you have failed or think you have failed in your quest for holiness. Ask for peace in your heart as you figure things out and learn that you are holy enough. Also ask to learn how to become more holy in ways that are best for you.

Pray about tomorrow.

Try this prayer: *Dear Lord, help me embrace the words of St. Francis de Sales to be who I am and to be that perfectly well. Help me pray more and try harder to be holy. But also help me see that there are many ways to be holy—and help me to find mine.*

11

Embracing Enough

*Do not fear what may happen tomorrow. The same loving Father
who cares for you today will care for you tomorrow and every day.
Either he will shield you from suffering or He will give you
unfailing strength to bear it. Be at peace then and put aside all
anxious thoughts and imaginings.*
—St. Francis de Sales

Imagine if you could no longer walk or talk or see. Are you still you?
Do you feel as if you are as important or lovable? Are you able to love
yourself just the way you are? Are you enough?

Knocked Off My Horse

It was a cool summer night, and it felt good to be helping my husband, John, with some yard work. I am not an outdoorsy person,
but I like to pitch in. We were clearing away some weeds and small
branches in the woods. I take a bit of pride in being a good worker
bee and was happy to haul debris. As we worked our way through
the woods, we noticed a tiny dead tree and I suggested we knock it
down so that there would be more room and clearer paths for the
grandchildren when they tromp around the mini forest. I guess I
was just feeling energized and wanted to do a bit more. My husband
agreed that the tree should go, so I marched through the grove, feeling
like a lumberjack as I trekked toward the dry, rotted piece of wood,

ready and a bit excited to push it to the ground. But my vision of woodsy fun never happened. A vine hidden under leaves wrapped itself around my ankle, and instead of the small tree being felled, I was. *Timber!* Down I went. Like St. Paul, I fell. And this fall awakened me.

First of all, the fall took me by surprise. I braced myself with my hands as I felt myself lose balance. I was too startled to have much time to react. The fall literally knocked the breath out of me, and I just lay on the floor of the forest. I was shaken and didn't comprehend what had just happened. The leaves in my hair and the pain in my wrist were pretty strong clues. So, after a few seconds, I pulled myself up from the dirt, sticks, and leaves and shouted for my husband, who came to help me up. My left wrist definitely hurt, but I figured it was only a sprain. Or at least I tried to convince myself it was only a sprain. Our daughter Kerry was visiting us, and she helped with ice and ibuprofen and kept insisting I seek medical treatment. I stubbornly refused to go to the doctor. This was not supposed to be how the beginning of my summer went. I did not want this kind of interruption or mess.

The next morning, my husband said, for the tenth time, that we should check out my wrist with an X-ray, just in case. I relented. I do not like going to the doctor, and I felt foolish for tripping, but I thought it would be best to quiet my family's chorus of "go to the doctor." I felt pleased when the physician assistant at the walk-in medical clinic said it just looked like a sprain. However, the X-rays told a different story. She said that her initial diagnosis was the one I wanted, but she had to tell me that I had a broken wrist. Her message made me feel fragile and sad and a little scared.

Fortunately, I was able to be seen by an orthopedic surgeon, and my wonderful husband drove me to all my medical visits that day. At our afternoon appointment, the very capable doctor put my wrist and arm in a cast, and we headed home. My granddaughter was disappointed that it was white instead of hot pink, but I let her draw on it, so that helped. I knew I was lucky and the fall could have been much worse. I could have hit my head. I could have required surgery. I could have broken a leg. I was mobile and not in much pain and being cared for by loved ones.

My head told me I was blessed to just have a broken wrist that did not require surgery. But I was not a grateful and happy camper. I was not sending up prayers of gratitude and feeling serene and trusting. No, I was as petulant as a toddler and focusing on the things I could not do. I could not make supper, and I like making food for our family. And our grandson Cillian was visiting, but I could not change his diaper. I could not even hold him. I like doting on the grandchildren and helping their parents. I was so frustrated. And I was mad that I had not seen the vine. I just wanted to do something. I did not want to sit with my arm raised over my heart and be told to read and relax. I love to read but did not want people to have to wait on me or help me. I was the mother, the grandmother, the maker of meals and holder of babies. I wanted to fulfill that role.

Then it hit me. This epiphany was as powerful as the fall that broke my wrist. I was a bit of a fraud. I thought I was so comfortable in my own skin and truly felt I had embraced what it means to feel enough. And I was partly right. I often felt content and did not worry too much about what others thought. I tried not to define myself by my job or my material possessions or intellect. And I know that sometimes my weight is up and sometimes it is down, and I focus on that a bit too much. I also realized that I was a good enough parent and was doing okay at being a decent person and a loving grandma. I was even willing to dance in my bathing suit if it made my grandchildren happy. So, I did it, right? I thought I could confidently say that I had embraced the fact that I was enough.

Nope.

Hurdles to Feeling Enough

Not yet. There were more hurdles. I still had some work to do.

My broken wrist really, really bothered me. It was not the pain. I did not feel that I needed medication. I needed to be whole. The heart of the matter was that I was upset with my inability to do things. My helplessness was my real discomfort.

My response seems so immature as I look back on it. Even at the time, I knew I was lucky. My husband washed my hair for me in the sink. We joked that I was at the salon. I had been forbidden to get the cast wet, so John helped me wrap a trash bag around my arm and secured it with rubber bands so I could take a modified bath. It was not bad at all, but I continued to be grumpy.

This experience made me realize just how much I needed to be useful. I organized the desk in our front hall and sorted all the birthday cards, stationery, sympathy cards, and manila envelopes. I cleared off a kitchen counter and threw away an array of ridiculous items and moved a ceramic cow planter to a better spot. In the cabinet filled with plastic containers, I reunited bottoms and covers. Ridiculously, I even tried knitting, but it was too painful. Another experiment was trying to type, but this led to one-handed poking at the keyboard. Rationally, I knew it was silly to resent my inability to do various tasks. Just a look around my small world revealed people facing far worse difficulties than mine. I could see so many hardships and illnesses that were permanent. No doubt about it, I was a bit of a crybaby. I knew I was being irrational, but I still felt the way I did. And I certainly did not feel *enough*.

My daughter Elizabeth, who had two children under the age of two at the time, tried to be a voice of reason. I like helping her, but she was now trying to help me in many ways, and I felt bad about that. She already had her hands full, and now she had to assist me with driving and everyday activities. I apologized to her and said that I was sorry I could not help her buckle her children into their car seats or carry them. I hated being helpless. She scoffed and, with her wonderful insight and wit, said, "Right, we only value people if they are useful." She pointed to her one-year-old son and said, "He needs a lot of help right now; is he useless?"

How Do You Define Yourself?

She is so smart and so right. And she made me see that although I do not define myself by my looks or possessions or accomplishments, I do like to be helpful. I like to take care of others. I like to bake and assist with the grandkids and do thoughtful things. If I could not do that anymore, who was I? And was that person enough? Did I feel I was enough if I was just me, maybe even a needy or helpless me?

My children and I had watched *Mister Rogers' Neighborhood* for years and are huge fans to this day. One of our favorite songs from the show is "It's You I Like." The lyrics conclude: "I hope that you'll remember, even when you're feeling blue, that it's you I like. It's you, yourself. It's you I like."

I always stressed that message to my children. I told them they were loved no matter what was on their report card. I told them we loved them if they struck out in a baseball game or broke a special piece of china. I believe it sincerely, and I love my children unconditionally. And I know God loves me that way, but I had not embraced that belief completely.

I knew the cast on my arm was temporary. I knew I would soon be back in my kitchen bustling about and making food. But I also knew that there would come a time when there would be no fix by a fiberglass cast. As I aged, I would become more dependent on others. Who would I be when I could no longer do much? Was I pretending to be enough or had I really arrived at the sense of contentment that can come from falling into the arms of God?

A True Selfie

Think of the times you take a selfie or look at a picture of yourself. What do you see? More importantly, whom do you see—beyond the physical attributes? Do you see yourself as a leader? Are you the person in the background offering food or decorations or organization? Are you the one who makes everyone laugh? Are you the good listener or the one with tales to tell? All those roles are wonderful and necessary and appreciated. But what if you could no longer do anything? Who would you be then? Are you ready to simply *be*? It is a frightening yet beautiful challenge.

The Grace of Old Age

When I was a young freelance reporter for the Catholic newspaper in Milwaukee, Wisconsin, I had been assigned to interview a Jesuit who had authored a book called *The Grace of Old Age.* I now wonder what Father Vincent M. O'Flaherty thought about the twenty-eight-year-old reporter who showed up to see him at the nursing home. I came not only with a pad and pen but also with an infant in a stroller. My job was to profile the priest and pass on his message about how one copes with old age.

He spoke to me about the nature of old age and the redemptive qualities that come with it. He wrote:

> When a man gets old and his mind gets foggy, he cannot formulate flowery prayers. At the beginning of the countdown, he should start saying the prayer of simple presentation so that he will be in the habit of using it when his faculties are not keen. . . . Push your wheelchair into the chapel and show your broken hip to the Lord. This throws the burden of giving you a cross on almighty God. It is the resigned way of praying with full resignation to the will of God.

As you can tell from the tone of the text, Father O'Flaherty did not see old age as rainbows, unicorns, and puppies. He saw it as a way to unite with God through suffering. He said he was not talking about "young" old age. Rather, this bright Jesuit was referring to the stage where you really cannot physically do much. Father O'Flaherty had been an author and a college professor. However, now he was living in a nursing home. He gave me a sad and sweet smile that seemed to say, "You really cannot understand." And I could not. I was beginning my life as a mom and a reporter. I was full of health and energy. He was trying to tell me and his readers that old age can bring one closer to God and make people more aware of why they exist.

That is no small insight. Being hobbled by a small accident gave me a glimpse into a life in which I would have limitations. I am not being morbid. I just realized that I may someday have an impairment that lasts longer than a month. I may someday be entirely dependent on others. Would I believe that I was enough then? I tried to sit in prayer but was restless. I told myself that God loves me in my mess and my weakness. I took comfort in the words of Pope Francis when he addressed the International Federation of Catholic Medical Associations in 2013. He said, "There is no human life more sacred than another, just as there is no human life qualitatively more significant than another."

Jesus, Pope Francis, and even Mr. Rogers say that we all are enough just the way we are. The message of our faith is that we are of value no matter our age or ability. The words of Pope Francis embraced me like the warm hug I needed at the time. And I hope they assure you that you are just fine, right here and right now.

I watched my own mother, who seemed to take care of the world when she was younger, sit daily and reach for a big Ziploc bag filled with prayer cards and novenas. She was an active and caring woman her whole life, but as she reached her late seventies she made even more time for prayer each day. And she seemed to realize that she could do good from her blue recliner as she spent time with God. When I was young, she would comfort me with the words, "There, there," and "It's okay." I love those phrases. I love the message that does not promise change. It does not make things better. It just sends love and hugs. My mother's presence, her faith, and her love came through in those words and have helped me love myself.

And now I say to you, "There, there; it's okay." When you are at your best or your worst, God loves you. You are loved. Whether you are sitting, standing, working, praying, wondering, wandering, questioning, loving, or dancing (maybe even in your bathing suit), know you are enough.

Saintly Inspiration

A wonderful example of a person who learned about changing roles and acceptance is a saint who is not a household name. She is St. Jeanne Jugan, and in 1839, at age forty-seven, she changed her life and the world. Before that day, she had lived a life of hard work and charity. She was a kitchen maid, a hospital worker, and a companion to an older woman. But now she was sharing a small home with a seventy-two-year-old woman and a seventeen-year-old orphan. Still, she felt she could do more to help others. With permission from her housemates, she gave up her bed to care for a blind widow. The group took in two more, and then it was forty elderly people in their care in a rented building. Others came to help, and the Little Sisters of the Poor religious community was founded.

She advised all who worked with her, "Be kind. Especially with the infirm. Love them well. Oh yes! Be kind. It is a great grace God is giving you. In serving the aged, it is [God] himself whom you are serving."

And St. Jeanne had to suffer herself. She became practically blind and was forced out of the leadership of her community to the extent that many did not know she was the founder. But she prayed and loved and lived a life of quiet prayer in her retirement.

Imagine a woman who cared so much for others being confined to doing nothing. That may be the fate of many of us. I fear losing my mental capacities and bringing grief to my loved ones. But I hope that, if there comes a point when I cannot lift a fork or my foot or even my voice in prayer, I will somehow know that I am still enough.

Putting Faith into Practice

- Many parishes have a program in which you can offer a ride to church for a senior member. Or maybe you could become a parish visitor to a nursing home or to a shut-in. This ministry is not easy, but it might open your eyes and heart.

- Finish this sentence: I am . . . Then reflect on your identity and ask yourself what it would mean if you could no longer be a teacher, parent, worker, or general helper.

- Look at people. Really look at them and smile. My granddaughter approached a little girl in a wheelchair at a parish picnic. The mother welcomed her greetings and her questions. While others looked away or maybe looked on with sadness, Cordelia saw a person and wanted to get to know her better.

- Send a note or a card to someone who has helped you. Focus on those who are older. Let them know that they matter and that you are grateful for their presence and their gifts.

Ignatian Examen

Give thanks.

Thank the Lord for the life you have right now and consider that as you sit or stand or use a walker or a hearing aid or glasses, you are enough. Thank the Lord you have lived the number of years you have lived. Be grateful for *being*.

Ask for the Spirit.

Ask the good Lord to help you see and appreciate the goodness in all people. Especially, look at those who need help throughout their day, whether physically or mentally. Someone might need an arm to lean on or a person willing to listen.

Review and recognize challenges and failures.

Have you feared being around old people because they make you think of what might be in your own future? Have you treated the elderly as burdens or needy people and not seen their basic humanity and dignity? Do you think that only useful people matter? Do you think you only matter if you are useful?

Ask for forgiveness and healing.

Lord, forgive me for ignoring people on the margins. Forgive me for being insensitive to the everyday struggles of so many people who work hard just to exist. Heal my heart from the fear of what is next and let me enjoy what is and who I am right now.

Pray about tomorrow.

Dear Lord, when I feel worthless, guide me to see myself as a valuable person in this world. And help me assure others that they are needed and wanted and valuable members of the community.

Closing Thoughts

Say this sentence out loud: "I am enough!"

Say it again: "I am enough."

Now focus on believing it in your mind and in your heart. I know that even now, there are days when I feel inadequate.

It is so hard to believe you are enough and valued by others and God. Somehow, all of us still seem to feel a little less than something.

We have seen it in the faces of older people who wonder if they have done enough in their lives.

We've heard it in the voices of parents who fret about doing enough for their families.

We've felt it in the frenzied pace of many more who are not sure if they are keeping up with others. And, most especially, we've heard it in the pained voices of young people who wonder if they will ever be pretty enough, smart enough, or popular enough.

And I want to wrap my arms around all of them and ask them to say aloud, "I am enough!" I want everyone to stop, take a really deep breath, and smile.

Then use your pen and paper or device one more time. Write these words: *I am enough as I am.* Maybe write it one more time. This should bring a smile. Then put that message on a mirror or bulletin board or post it on your computer screen. Remind yourself every day that you are truly enough as you are.

We may not be the richest or the smartest person in the world. And maybe we are not the best looking or the holiest or the friendliest. That's okay. We need to adjust our hearing and listen to the voices that really matter, the voices of those who love us—especially the voice of God.

I look again to St. Francis de Sales and find comfort as he writes: "Grace is never wanting. God always gives sufficient grace to whoever is willing to receive it."

I do not always believe that God's grace is sufficient and that God would love me if he really knew me. I can be petty. I can hold a grudge. I gossip. Sometimes I'm lazy. And then I think again. Maybe it is through the grace of God that God knows all those things about me and still loves me. That is amazing and scary and wonderful.

I do know this: if you and I truly believed that we are enough, simply as children of God, then we would be a lot happier and we would be able to see others in a more positive and loving way.

I encourage you to say, "I am enough as I am," upon waking and before sleeping.

Turn to your loved ones, colleagues, and strangers and think, *You are already enough.* If it's a good time to say it out loud, do that. Not only can we heal ourselves by learning to believe this truth, but we can help heal others as well.

Acknowledgments

Having this book published is a true blessing and fulfillment of a dream.

Of course, this project was not done alone, and it is because of the support of so many people that it is possible.

So here goes.

Thanks always, to John.

Thanks to my parents, Hank and Connie Martin, who gave me my first electric typewriter, my faith, and a listening ear to my stories.

To my son, Matthew, who was my advocate and promoter, and his wife, Nell, who encouraged me.

To my daughter Kerry, who used her editor's eye to assist me.

To my daughter Elizabeth, who made so many helpful suggestions and reminded me to breathe when I write.

To Joellyn Ciciarelli, the president of Loyola Press, who gave this book a chance.

To the incredibly talented group at Loyola Press who showed me the ropes and created a great cover, layout, promotion, and product: Thank you, Maria Cuadrado, Vinita Wright, Carrie Freyer, Mandy Lemos, and Kelly Hughes.

To Joe Durepos, who guided me at the beginning of this book.

To my colleagues at Catholic Communications in the Diocese of Springfield, who will always be my friends and who helped me grow as a writer.

To Marquette University, where I learned to combine my love of faith and writing.

To Providence College, a truly special place that nurtured my faith and my thinking.

To all my friends and family who have led me to this place today.

About the Author

Peggy Weber is an award-winning journalist and author who has been working at her craft for almost 40 years, primarily with the Catholic press. The author of the popular "Spun from the Web" column, she loves her faith, family, baseball, and chocolate, not necessarily in that order. She loves to laugh a lot—often at herself—which helps her to truly feel "enough." She lives in Western Massachusetts with her dear husband, John, and relishes frequent visits from her seven grandchildren.

Other Women's Spirituality Books

Want to read more books like *Enough as You Are?* Check out these other books for women's spirituality.

Small Simple Ways

BY VINITA HAMPTON WRIGHT

The reflections in this daily devotional will help you discover "God in all things," recognize the graces of the day, and take simple, powerful steps towards a healthy spiritual life.

Paperback | 978-0-8294-4541-1 | $14.95

Busy Lives & Restless Souls

BY BECKY ELDREDGE

Written from the experience of a young, busy woman, you'll discover a fresh perspective on how to satisfy your restlessness within by making space for prayer amid a demanding life.

Paperback | 978-0-8294-4495-7 | $13.95

A Catholic Woman's Book of Days

BY AMY WELBORN

This daily devotional is written specifically for the unique experience of Catholic women as they develop a rich relationship with God, their faith, and the Church.

Paperback | 978-0-8294-2057-9 | $12.95

To Order:

Call **800.621.1008**, visit **loyolapress.com/store**, or visit your local bookseller.

Other Books by the Weber Family

Mercy in the City

BY KERRY WEBER

A young, single woman lives a "regular" life amid the daily pressures of New York City, while also living a life devoted to service and practicing real works of mercy.

Paperback | 978-0-8294-3892-5 | $13.95

Operating on Faith

BY MATT WEBER

This true story follows a newly married man as he shares how a loving God, a selfless wife, and a sense of humor carried him through the most difficult year of his life.

Paperback | 978-0-8294-4409-4 | $13.95

Fearing the Stigmata

BY MATT WEBER

Wit, earnest candor, and great storytelling illustrates for young adult Catholics the real challenges and immense joys of publicly living out the Catholic faith.

Paperback | 978-0-8294-3736-2 | $13.95

To Order:

Call **800.621.1008**, visit **loyolapress.com/store,** or visit your local bookseller.

Bjenkins@my.centenaryj.edu